BASIC SWEATER, KNITTED IN STOCKINETTE STITCH

Prepare the followings.

MATERIALS: Bulky yarn, (100% wool, 2oz.=98yds): Brown, 540g.
EQUIPMENT: Knitting needles: No. 8 (5.1mm), one set of two; No. 7 (4.5mm), one set each of two and four. Crochet hook, size 4/E (3.5mm). Tapestry needle. Stitch holders. Markers.

This sweater is knitted in basic stitches. Follow the step-by-step instructions of the book, and you can make the sweater quite easily. After this, you are ready to challenge next project.

GAUGE

16 sts = 10cm; 20 rows = 10cm in stockinette st.

Back

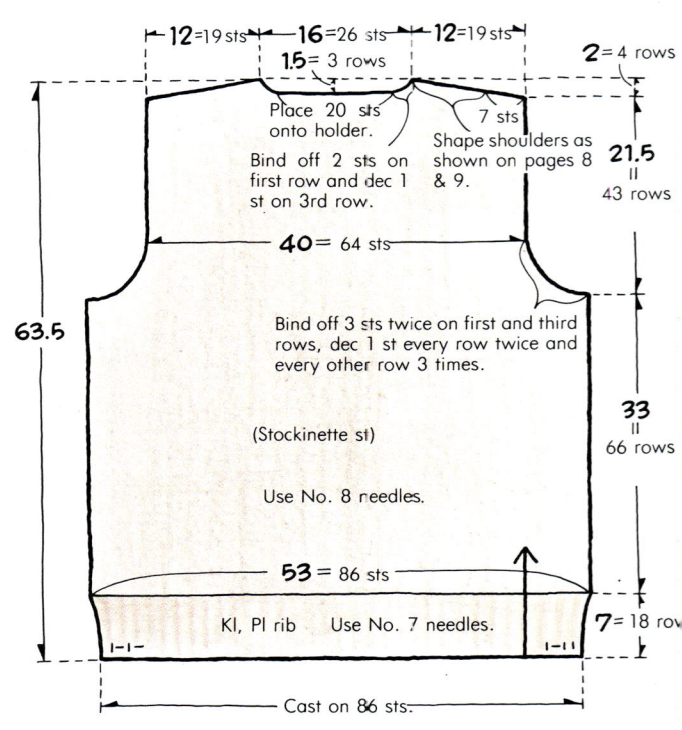

How to check gauge

Make a piece of knitting 15-20cm square, using some yarn and needles you are going to work with for the project. Block this sampler and count number of stitches and rows within center 10cm square of the sampler. This is the gauge of 10cm. When you work in pattern stitch, make a sample in pattern st and check gauge.
If stitches are tighter, change the needles to larger size and if looser, change them to smaller size. Always try to get the right gauge as indicated.

Finished size

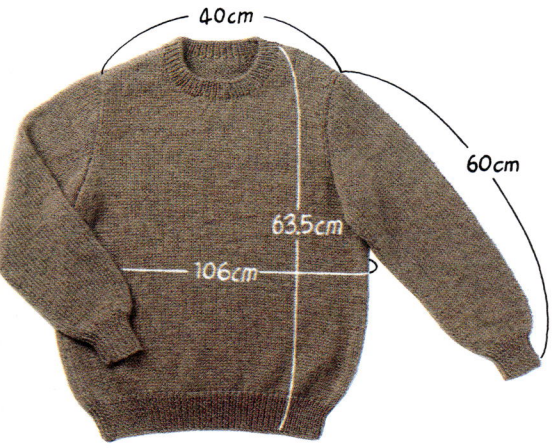

(1) Cast on 86 sts.

Using No. 8 needle, cast on 86 sts. Fold yarn 200cm from the end and start casting on, holding yarn over thumb and forefinger of left hand.

General method of casting on

This is the easiest and most common method and cast-on sts have some elasticity. Use single knitting needle, two sizes larger than the needles to be used for rib. Measure yarn three and a half times as long as the width of bottom edge and make a slip knot at that point. Hold yarn over thumb and forefinger. Cast-on sts are counted as first row of knit st.

1 Hold yarn over forefinger. Two sizes larger than needles to be used for rib. Leave yarn end three and a half times as long as width of bottom edge. Hold shorter yarn over thumb.

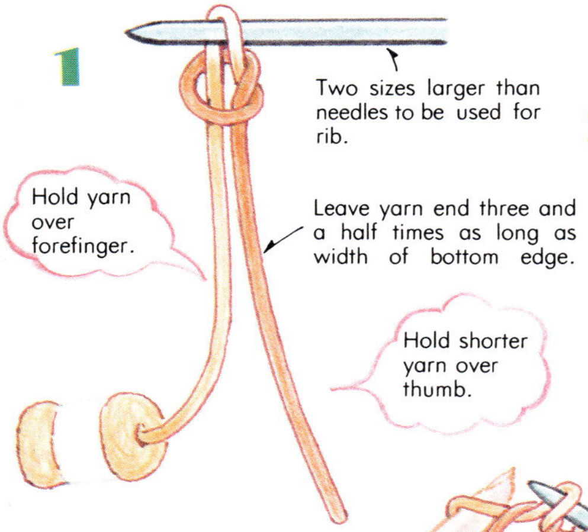

2 Shorter yarn

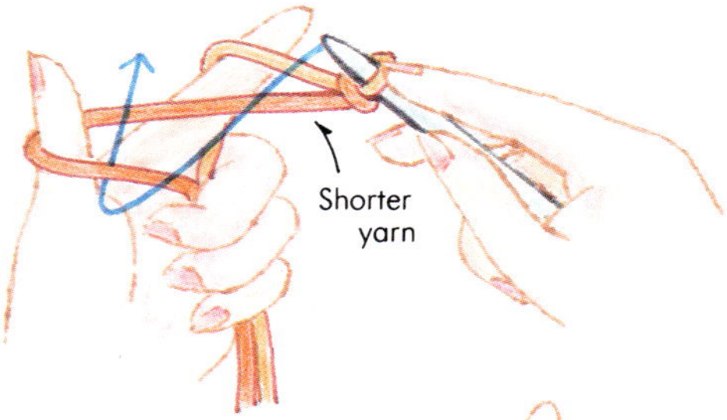

3

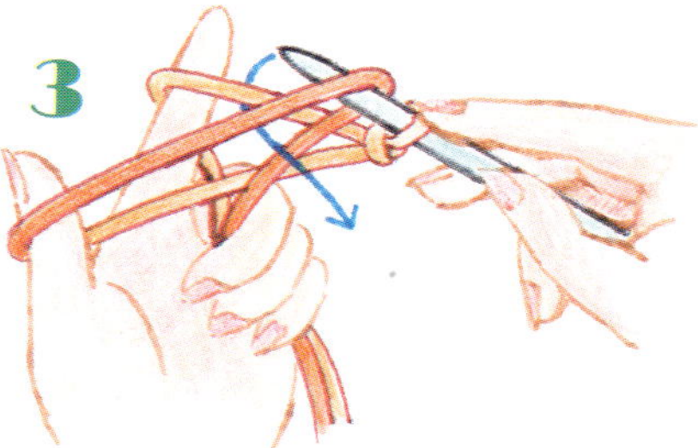

4 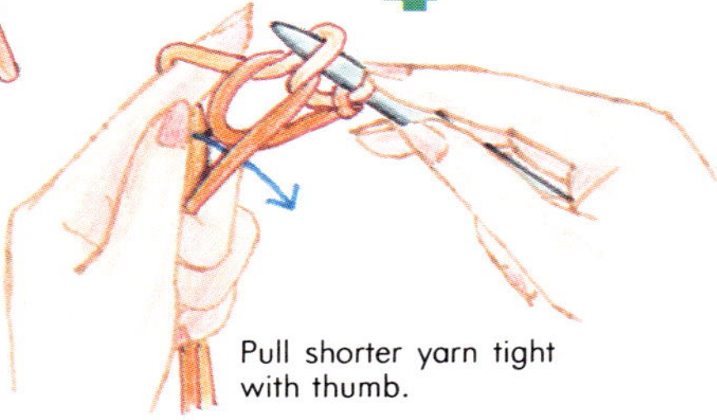 Pull shorter yarn tight with thumb.

5 Don't cast on too tight.

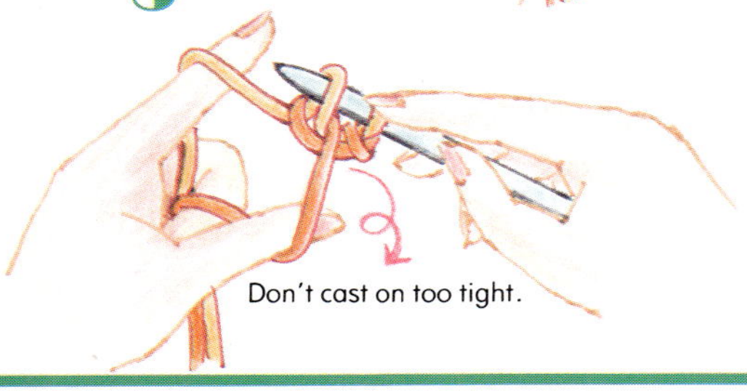

6 Repeat steps 2-5. Count these sts as one row of knit stitch.

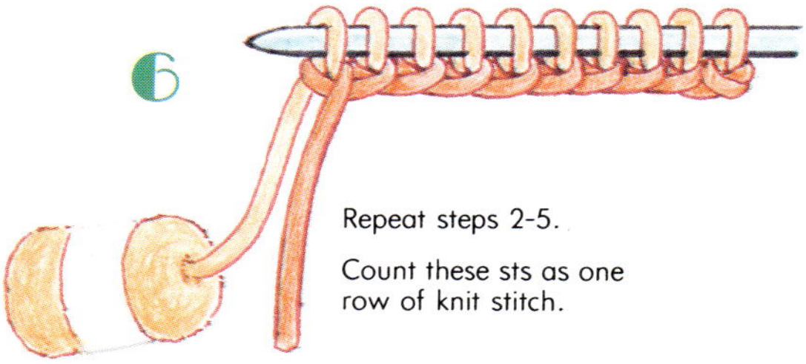

(2) Work in K1, P1 rib.

The first row of rib is made by casting on, so start working from second row. Repeat K1 and P1 alternately with No. 7 needles, but work K2 at right side and K1 at left side on front (P1 at right side and P2 at left side on wrong side). Turn and work with wrong side facing on even rows, so reverse the chart, that is, P for K and vice versa on the chart. Work following chart on uneven rows. Work even to 18th row in this manner.

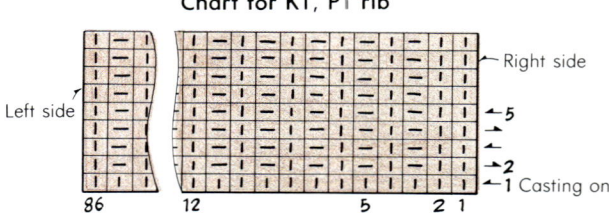

Chart for K1, P1 rib

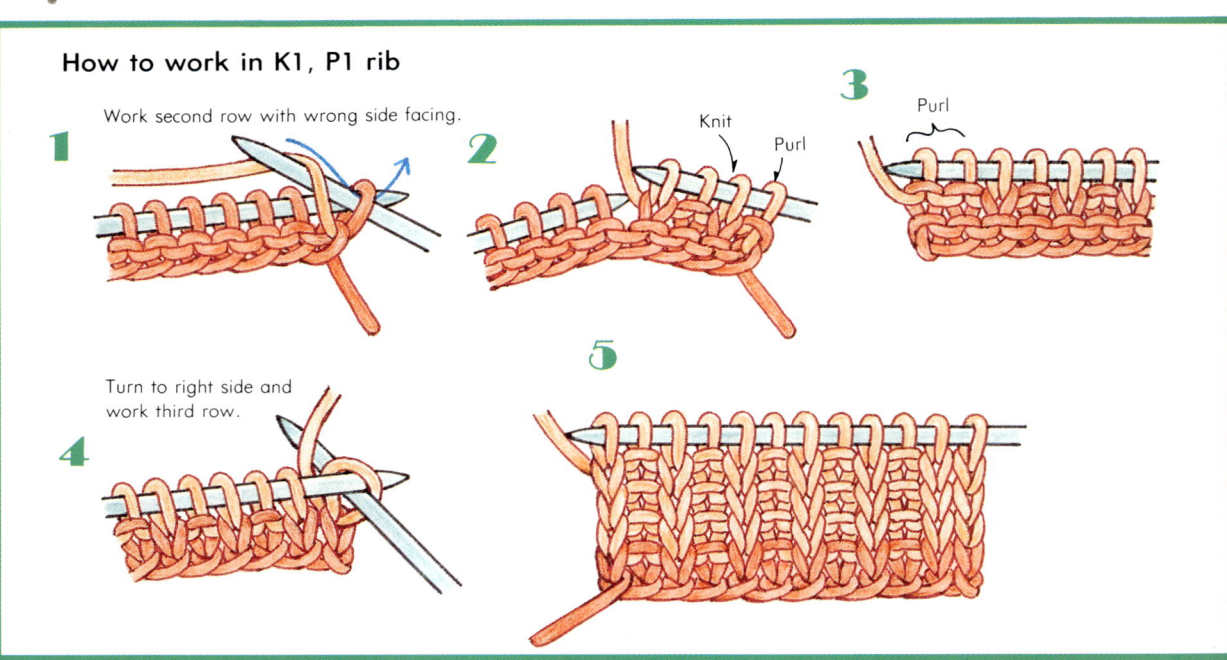

How to work in K1, P1 rib

How to hold needles and yarn

Hold yarn over forefinger of right or left hand as shown on the right. Use the method easier for you to hold and work with yarn and try to make even stitches.
How to hold yarn over left hand:
Hold yarn over forefinger of left hand. Keep yarn taut but let it move smoothly as you knit.
How to hold yarn over right hand:
Hold yarn over forefinger of right hand. Bring yarn away from yourself over right needle each time you knit.

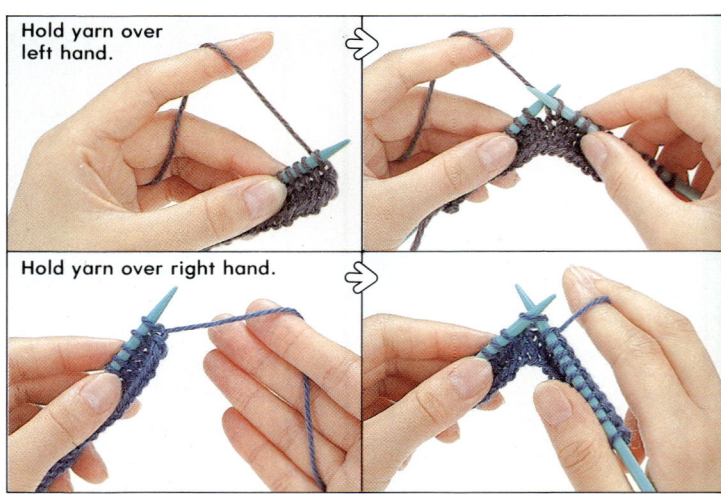

(3) Work even to 66th row.

Change to No. 8 needles and work even to 66th row in st st.

How to join yarn

Try to join a new ball of yarn at the beginning of a row for a neater finish. Leave old yarn at the end of row and join new one leaving 4-5cm without tying knot. After working several rows, tie ends of new and old yarn, weave ends into stitches and trim excess.

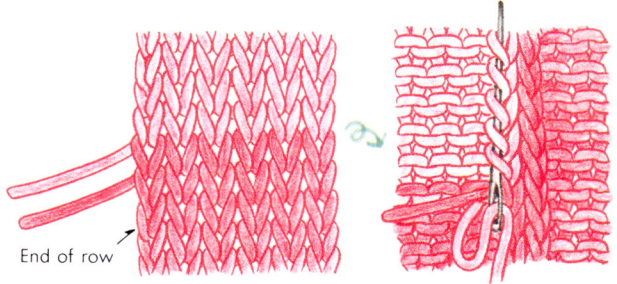

End of row

Weave ends into stitches

▯ How to knit

Right

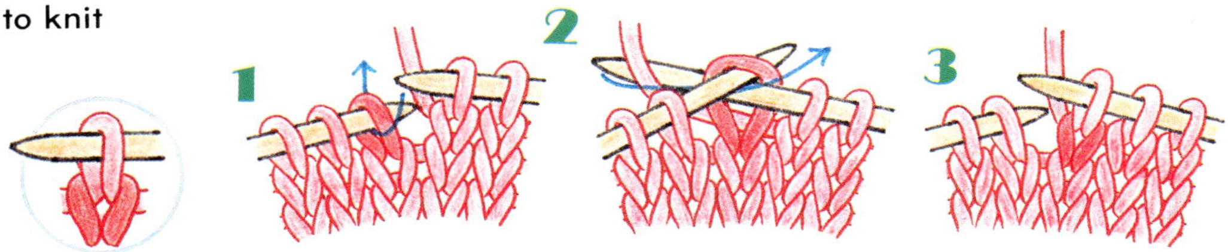

Wrong

If the needle is inserted in wrong way …

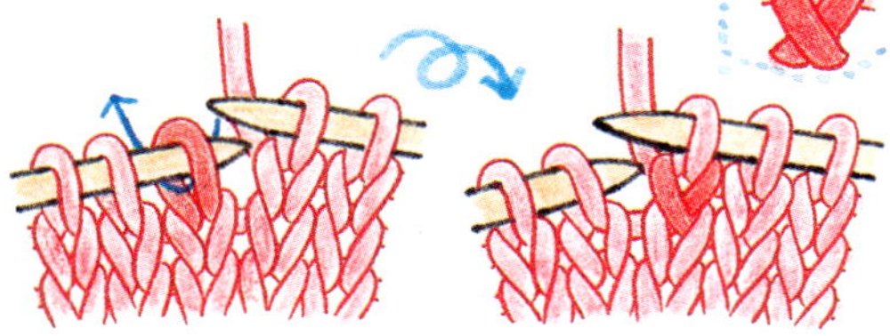

If yarn is brought over in wrong way …

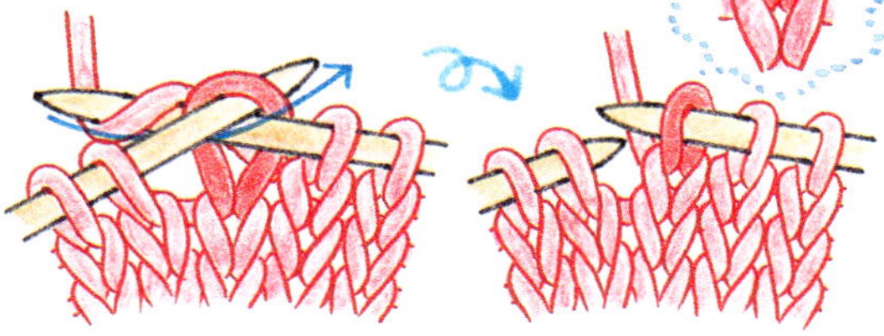

▬ How to purl

Right

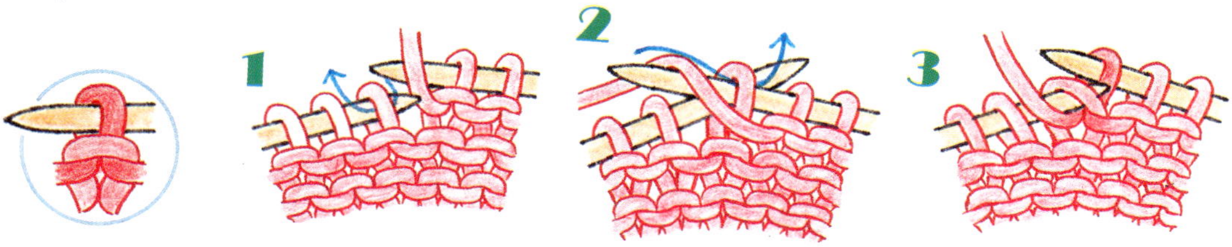

Wrong

If yarn is brought over in wrong way …

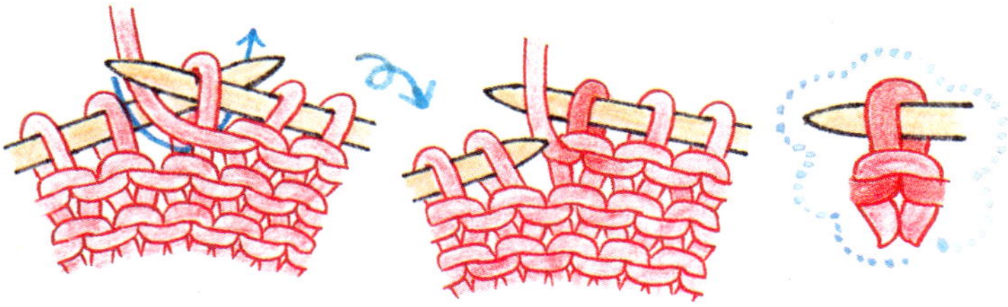

The stockinette stitch is produced when working knit and purl rows alternately.

The reverse stockinette stitch is the purl side of stockinette stitch.

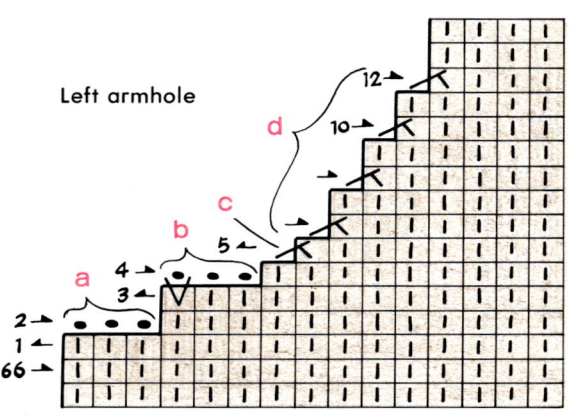

Left armhole

How to decrease for shaping left armhole

To decrease more than 2 sts

(a) To angle the corner

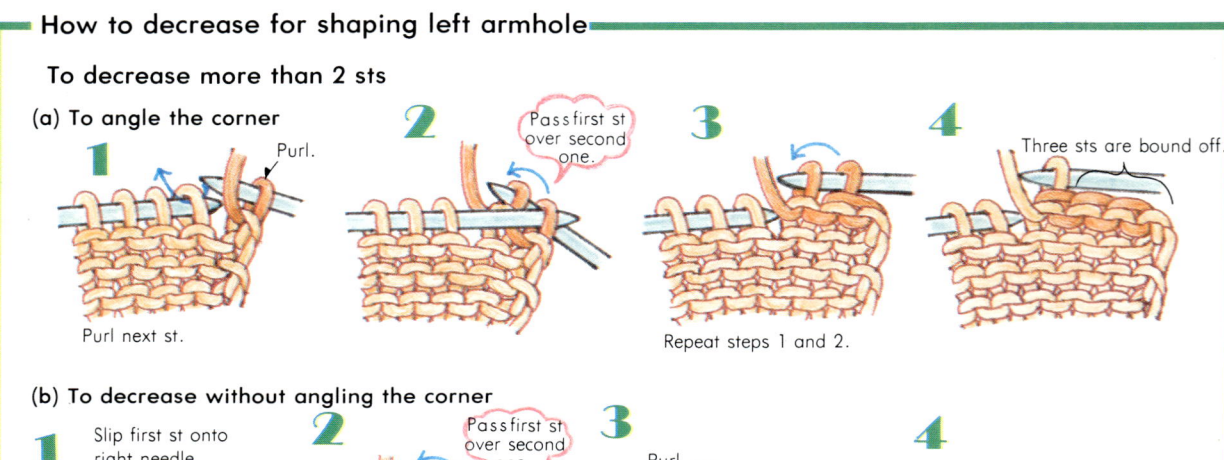

1. Purl next st. Purl.
2. Pass first st over second one.
3. Repeat steps 1 and 2.
4. Three sts are bound off.

(b) To decrease without angling the corner

1. Slip first st onto right needle. Purl next st.
2. Pass first st over second one.
3. Purl.
4.

To decrease one st

(c) K2 tog. (work with right side facing)

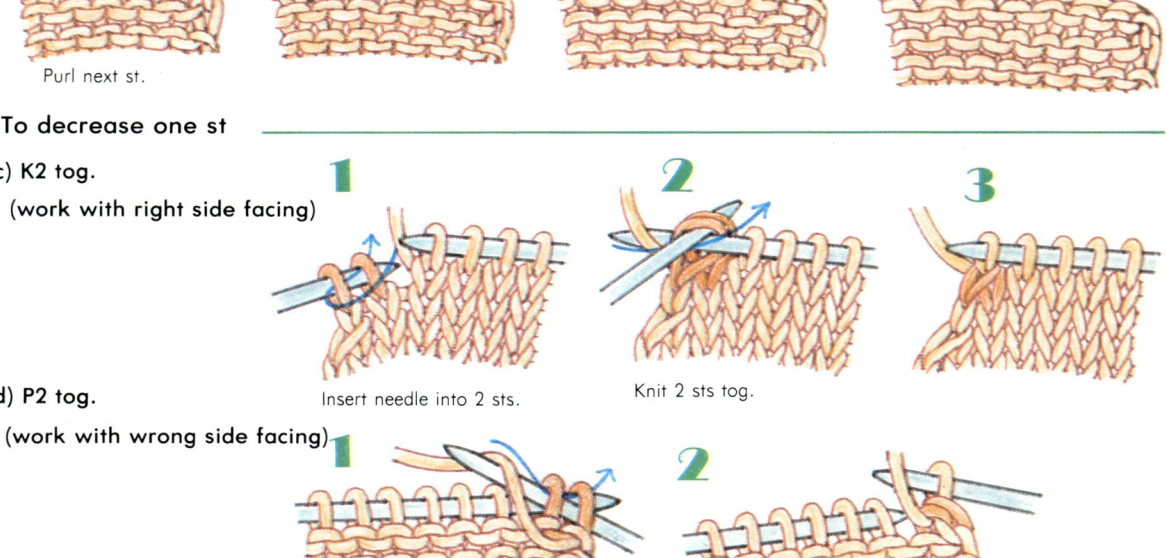

1. Insert needle into 2 sts.
2. Knit 2 sts tog.
3.

(d) P2 tog. (work with wrong side facing)

1. Purl 2 sts tog.
2.

(4) Shape armholes.

Bind off 3 sts with the method (a) shown on opposite page. Work even on second row. Bind off 3 sts with the method (b) on third row. From 4th row, dec one st as shown on chart. There is one row difference between right and left sides for decreasing. Start decreasing from 2nd row on left side. Don't knit too tight when decreasing. Bind off loosely when you do more than 2 sts. After shaping armholes, work even to 43rd row.

*You can decrease more than 2 sts on the side where there is a ball of yarn.

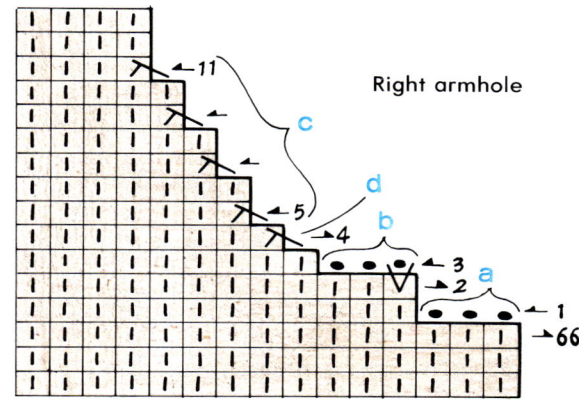

Right armhole

How to decrease for shaping right armhole

To decrease more than 2 sts

(a) To angle the corner

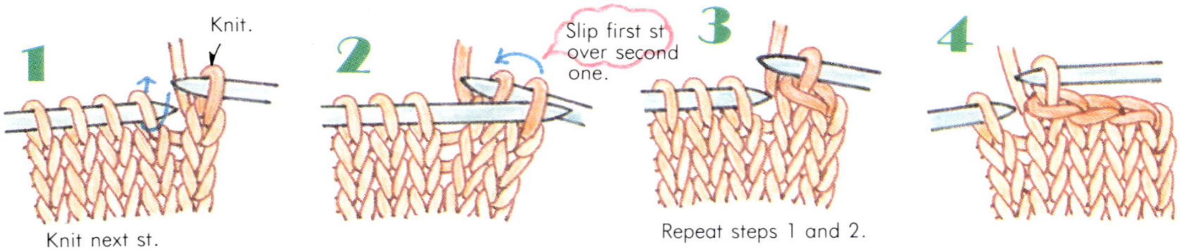

1. Knit.
2.
3. Slip first st over second one.
4. Repeat steps 1 and 2.

Knit next st.

(b) To decrease without angling

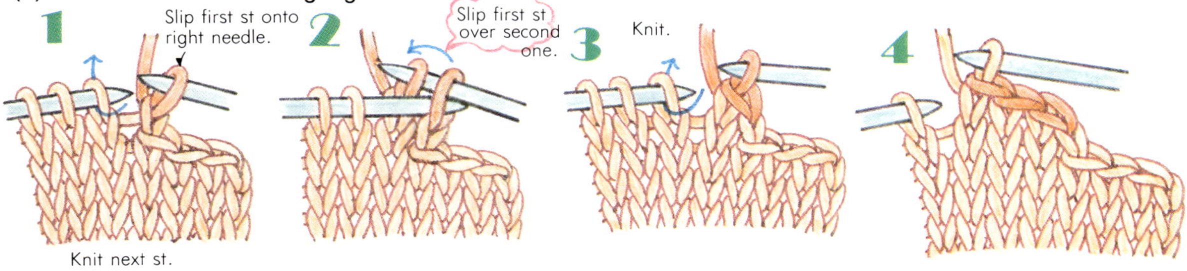

1. Slip first st onto right needle.
2. Slip first st over second one.
3. Knit.
4.

Knit next st.

To decrease one st

(c) Slip one st, knit 1, psso
 (work with right side facing).

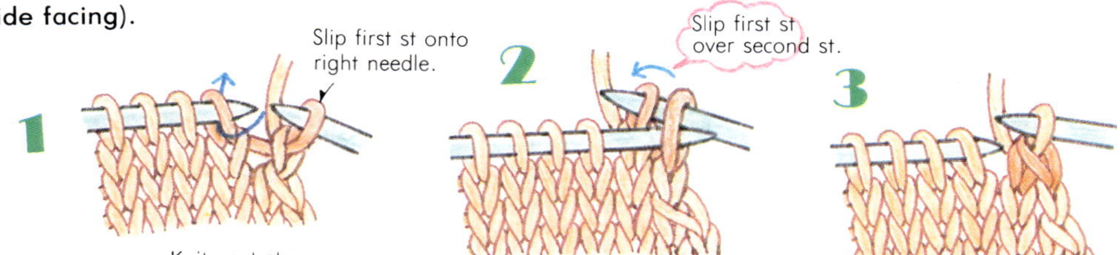

1.
2. Slip first st onto right needle.
3. Slip first st over second st.

Knit next st.

(d) Purl 2 sts tog.
 (work with wrong side facing)

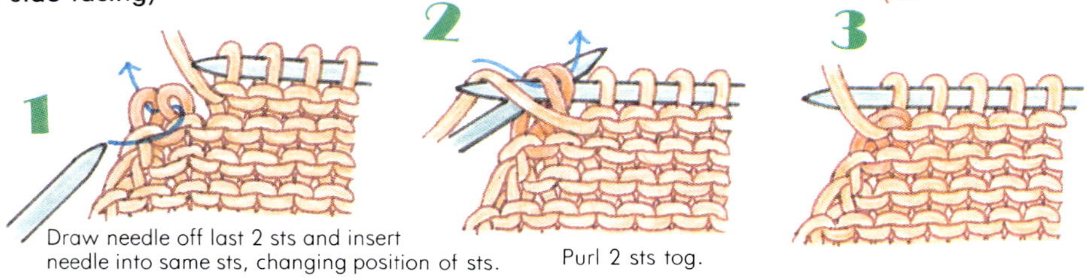

1.
2.
3.

Draw needle off last 2 sts and insert needle into same sts, changing position of sts. Purl 2 sts tog.

(5) Shape shoulders and neck.

After shaping armholes and working even to 43rd row, shape shoulders and neck. Work for right shoulder first.

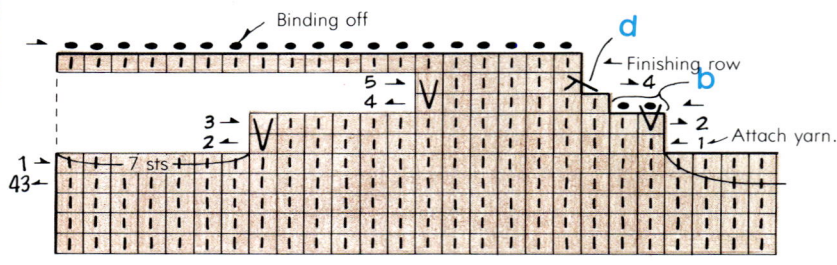

How to shape shoulder (left side)

1 Leave 7 sts on left needle without knitting.
Attach yarn at right side (first row of neck edge) and work until there are 7 sts left on left needle.

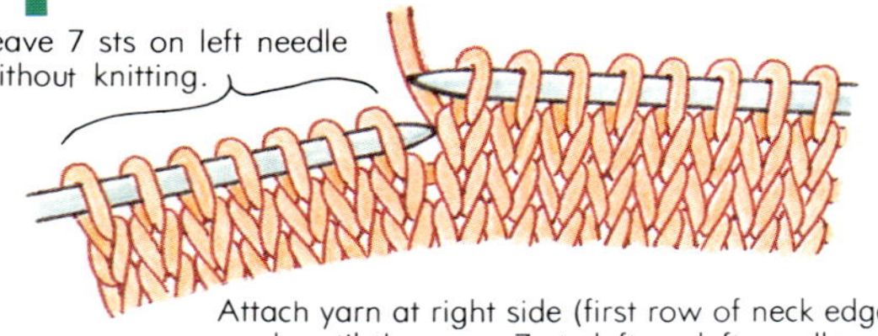

2 Slip st. 7 sts
Turn to wrong side. Mark with a thread and slip one st onto right needle and work 3rd row.

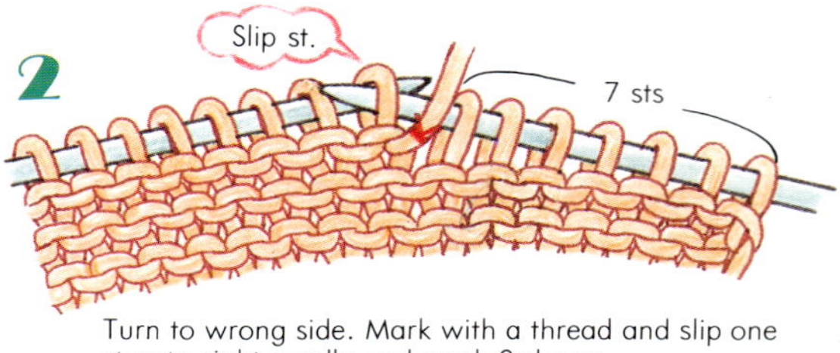

3 Leave 6 sts.
Turn to right side and work 4th row leaving 6 sts on left needle.

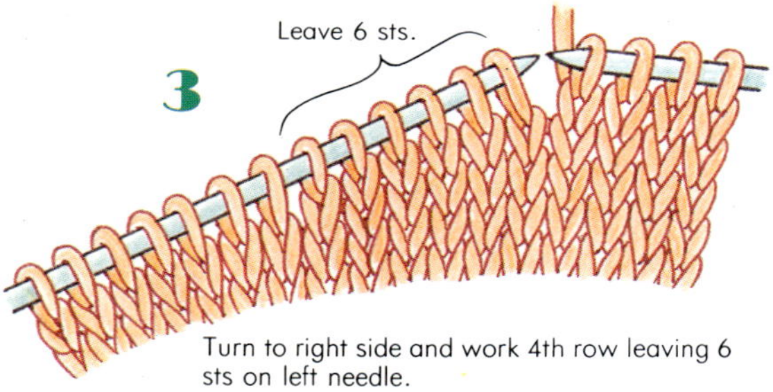

4 Slip st.
Turn to wrong side. Slip one st onto right needle and work 5th row.

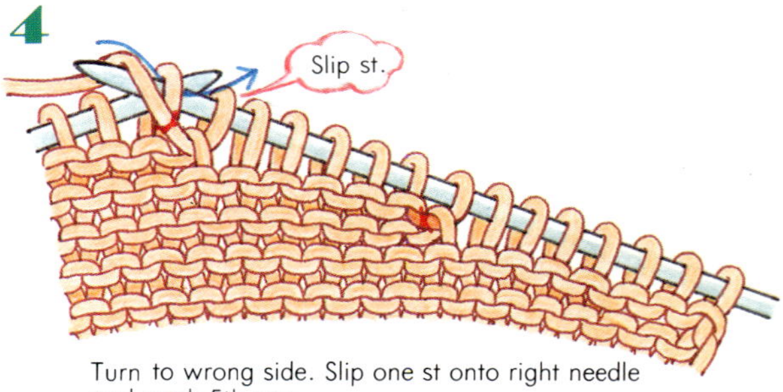

5 Pick up slipped st with mark onto left needle and knit 2 sts tog.

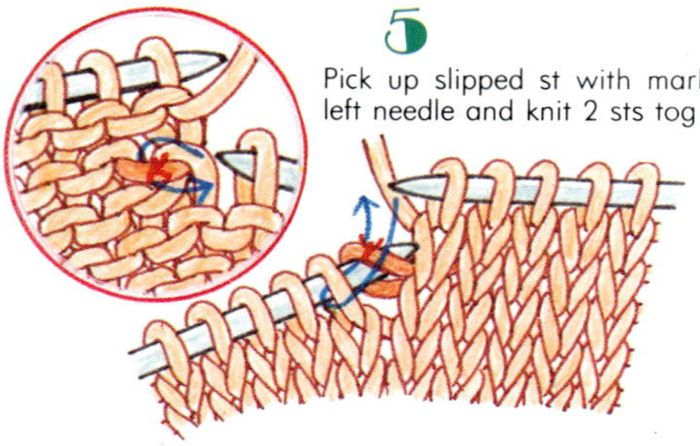

Finishing

After shaping shoulder, work last row with right side facing for closing gaps caused by turns. When you come to slipped st with mark, pick up the stitch onto left needle and knit this and next st together to prevent holes.

6 Wrong side

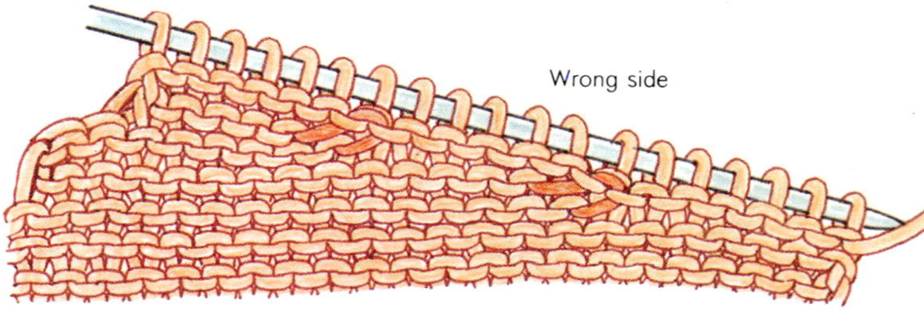

Work for right shoulder first.
Start to make right shoulder with wrong side facing (purl row). Work in reverse st st until there are 7 sts left on left needle. Turn to right side. Slip first st and knit next sts, place next 20 sts at center back onto a holder with the 22 remaining sts for left shoulder. Shape right shoulder as shown below and at the same time shape neck. Bind off all the stitches after finishing row is worked.
Work left shoulder in same manner as for right but start from neck edge attaching new yarn.

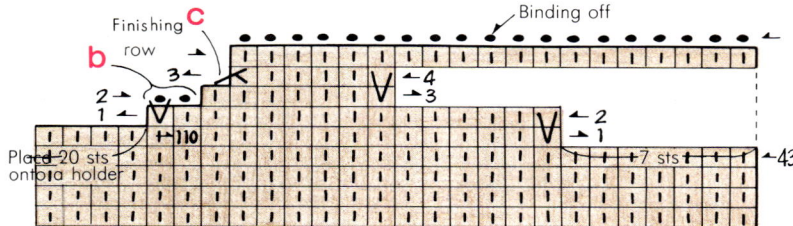

How to shape shoulder (right side)

1 Leave 7 sts.

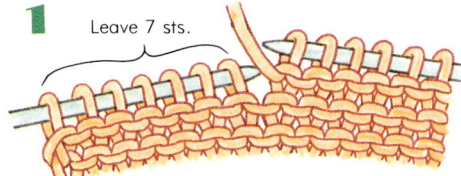

Leave 7 sts on left needle without knitting.

2 Slip st.

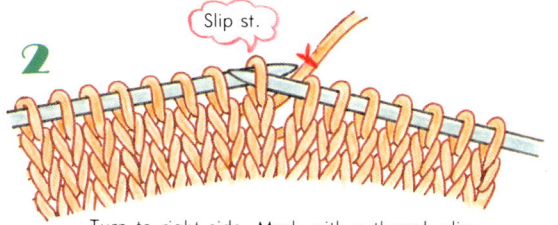

Turn to right side. Mark with a thread, slip one st onto right needle and knit second row.

3 Leave 6 sts.

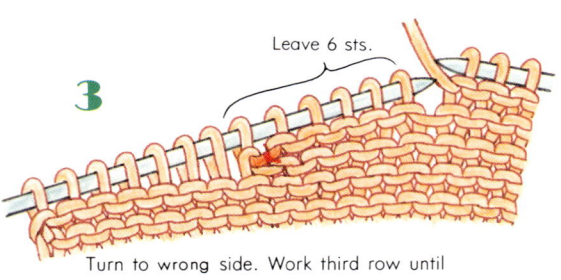

Turn to wrong side. Work third row until there are 6 sts left on left needle.

4 Slip st.

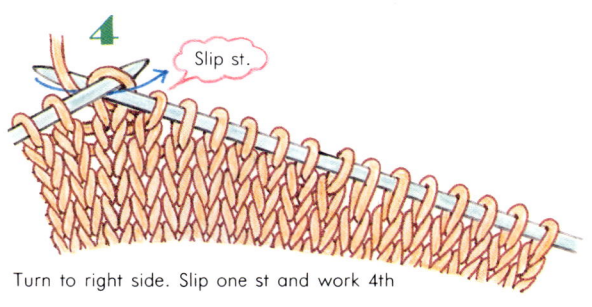

Turn to right side. Slip one st and work 4th row.

Finishing

After shaping shoulder, work last row with wrong side facing to close gaps caused by turns. When you are 6 sts from the beginning of the row, drop one st from left needle, pick up marked st onto left needle, then pick up dropped st, and purl 2 sts together to prevent holes.

5 Drop one st from left needle, pick up slipped st and then pick up dropped st.

Purl 2 sts together.

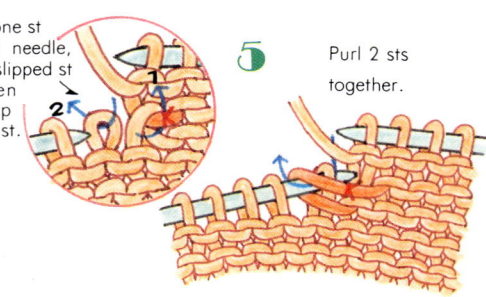

6 Wrong side.

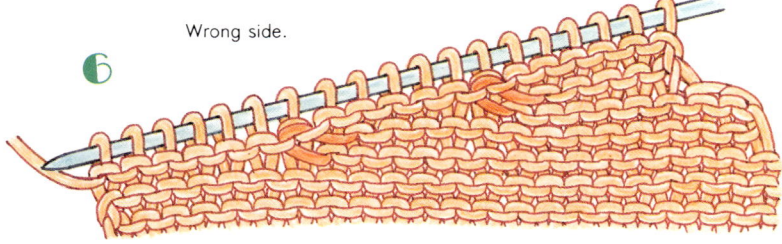

See next page for binding off.

(6) Bind off all the stitches of shoulders.

Bind off all the stitches of shoulders, after shaping.
Using crochet hook, bind off loosely.

Binding off (right shoulder)

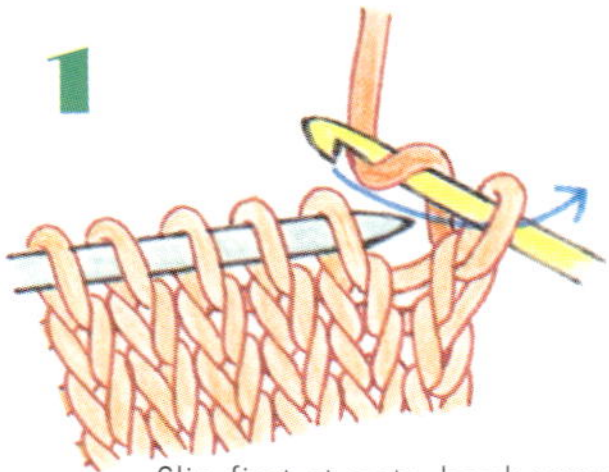

1. Slip first st onto hook, yarn over hook and draw yarn through first st. 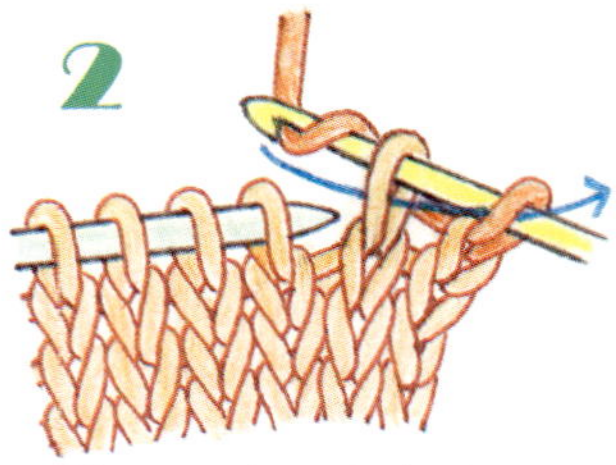
2. Slip second st onto hook, yarn over hook and draw yarn through 2 sts.
3. Draw yarn purlwise.

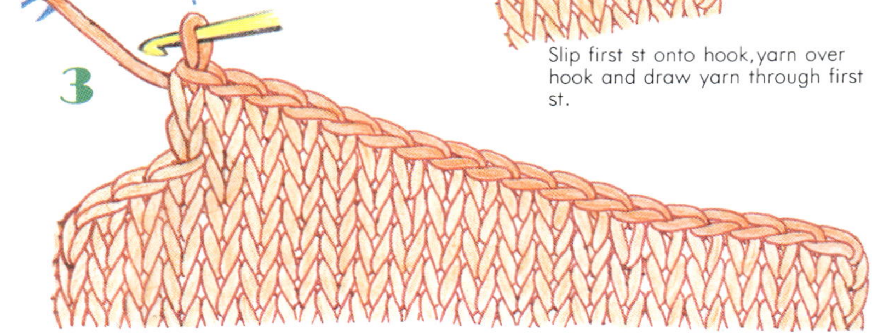

(left shoulder)

Draw yarn through sts.

Right side

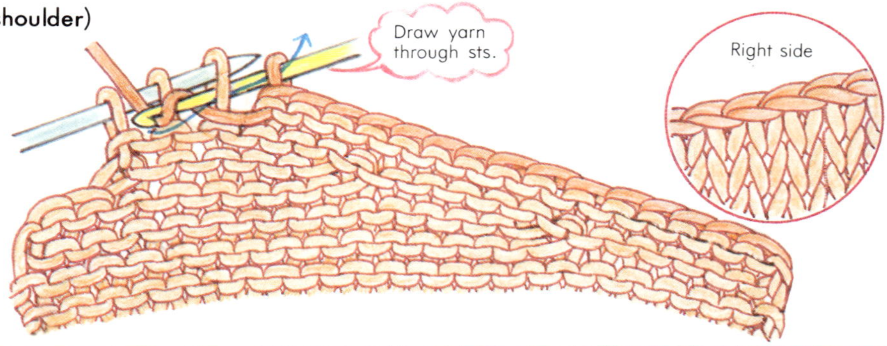

Chart for shaping neck and shoulders

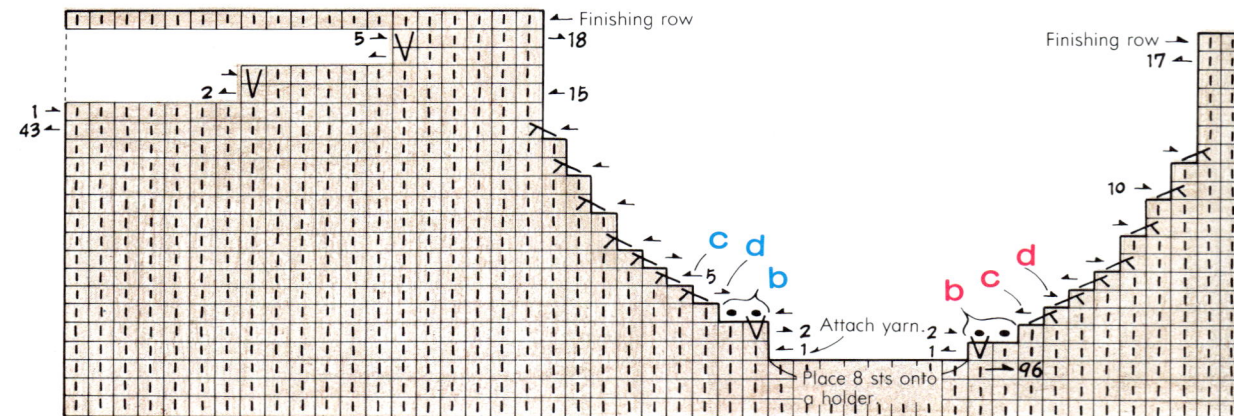

Front

(1) Work for front from bottom to neck.

Work for front as for back. Cast on 86 sts. Work in K1, P1 rib for 18 rows, then work in st st to 66th row. Shape armholes and work to 33rd row.

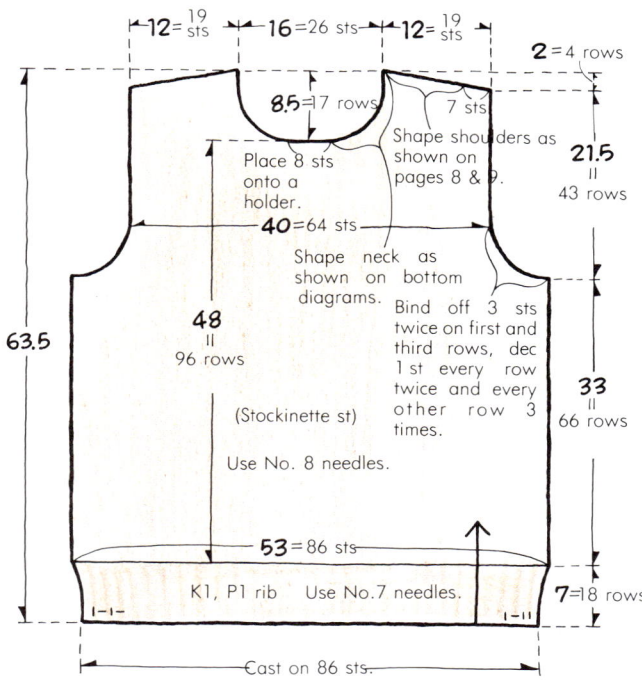

(2) Shape neck and shoulders.

Work left shoulder first.

After working to center of 31st row above bound-off sts, place 8 sts at center front onto a holder and hold 28 sts on needle for right shoulder. Shape neck edge decreasing as shown on the chart on opposite page from center front neck to 13th row, then start shaping right shoulder in same manner as for back (see page 9). After working finishing row, leave all the stitches on needle and about 3cm of yarn.

Work for right shoulder.

Attach yarn at the beg of first row and work in same manner as for left shoulder (see page 8).

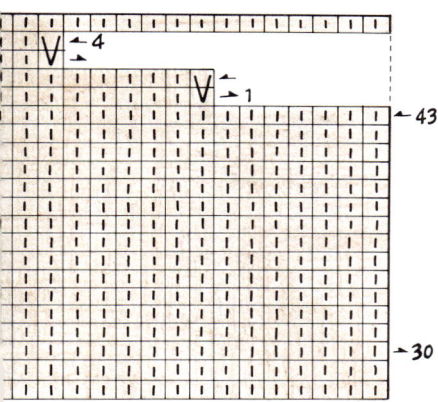

Sleeves

(1) Cast on 40 sts and work in K1, P1 rib.

Cast on 40 sts in same manner as for body and work in K1, P1 rib to 18th row.

(2) Work for sleeve.

Inc 8 sts evenly spaced (= 48 sts) as shown after working in rib. Work in st st to 80th row increasing one st at each side following chart.

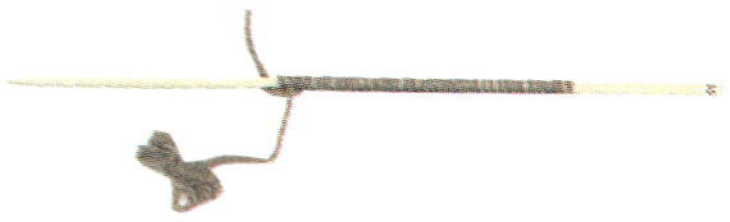

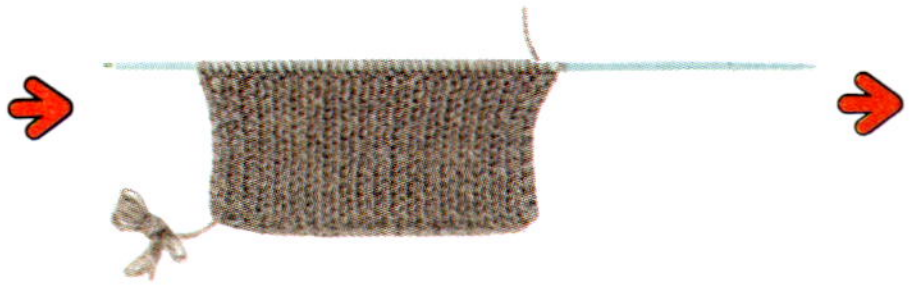

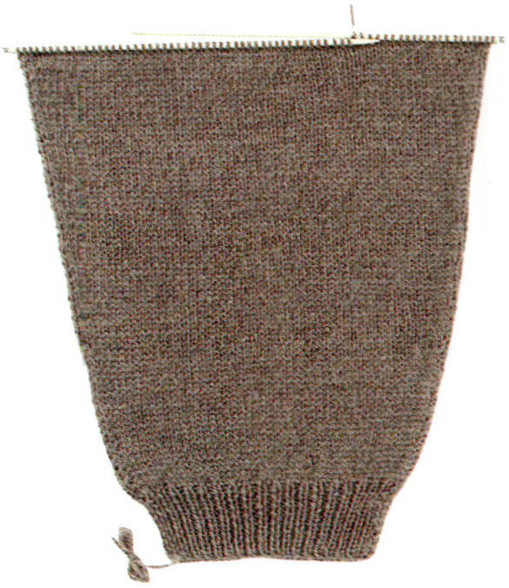

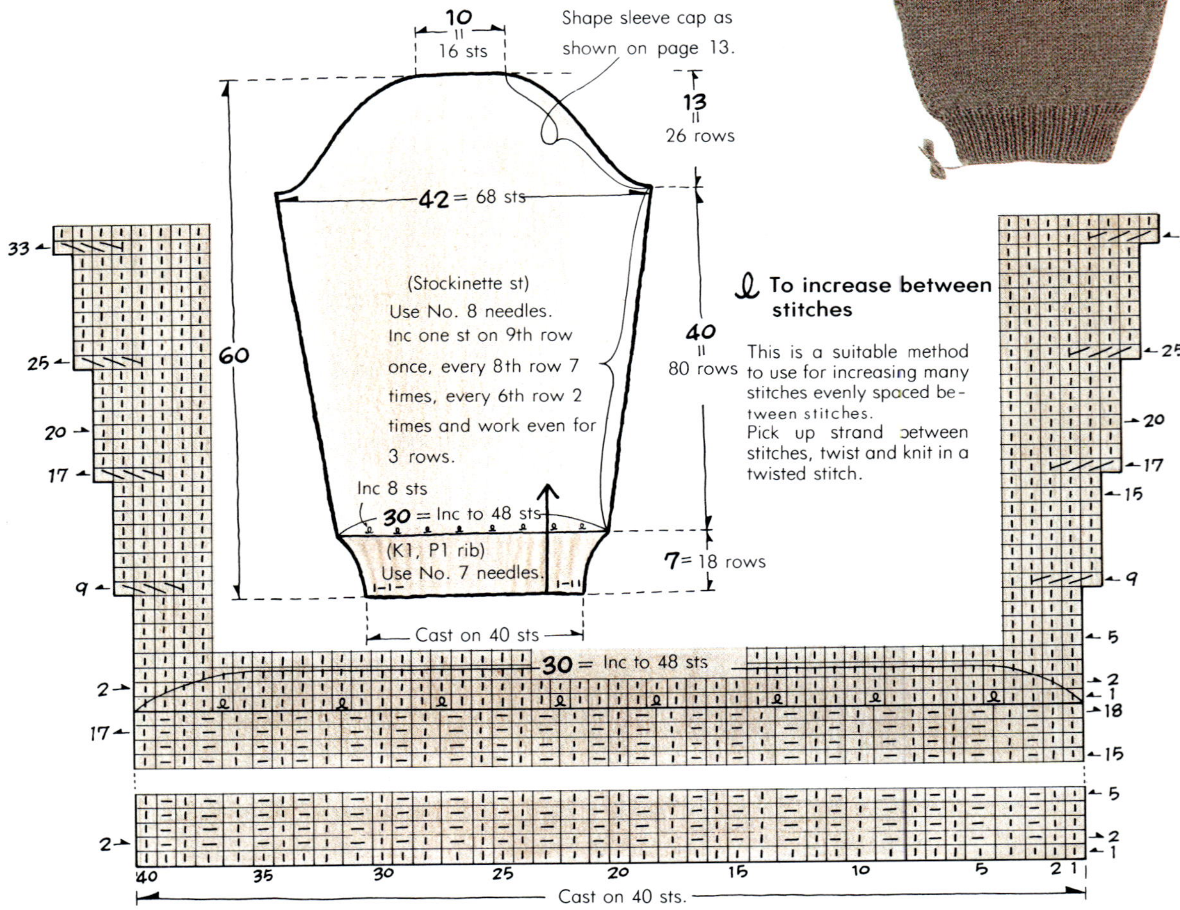

(Stockinette st)
Use No. 8 needles.
Inc one st on 9th row once, every 8th row 7 times, every 6th row 2 times and work even for 3 rows.

Inc 8 sts
30 = Inc to 48 sts
(K1, P1 rib)
Use No. 7 needles.

Shape sleeve cap as shown on page 13.

ℓ To increase between stitches

This is a suitable method to use for increasing many stitches evenly spaced between stitches.
Pick up strand between stitches, twist and knit in a twisted stitch.

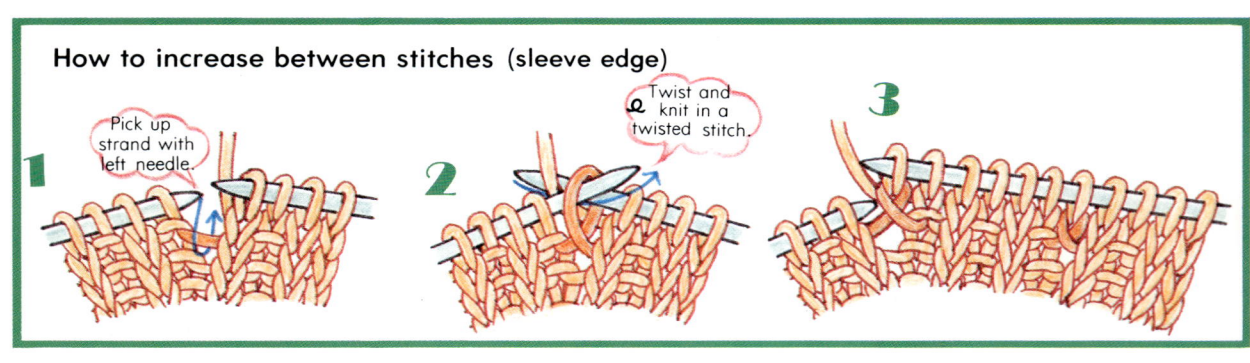

How to increase between stitches (sleeve edge)

1. Pick up strand with left needle.
2. Twist and knit in a twisted stitch.
3.

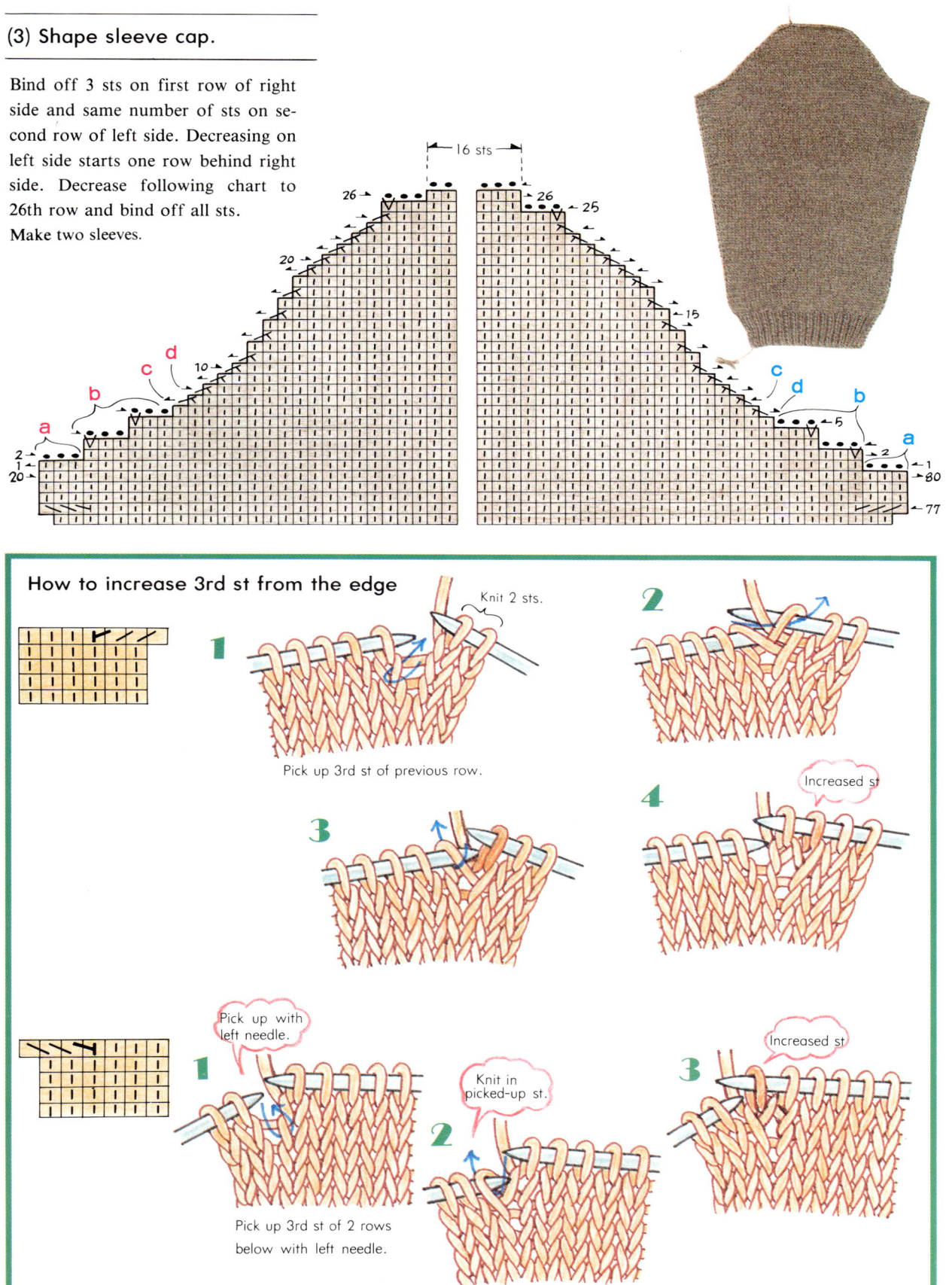

Finishing

(1) Block knitting pieces with steam iron.

Block front, back and sleeves with steam iron.
Place knitting on ironing pad with wrong side up. Pin around knitting adjusting to the size as given in the directions.

How to block

(2) Join shoulder seams.

Using remaining yarn, join shoulder seams, matching front and back shoulders.

How to thread

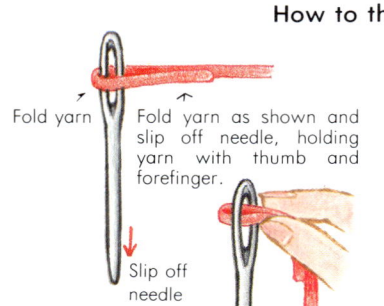

How to graft

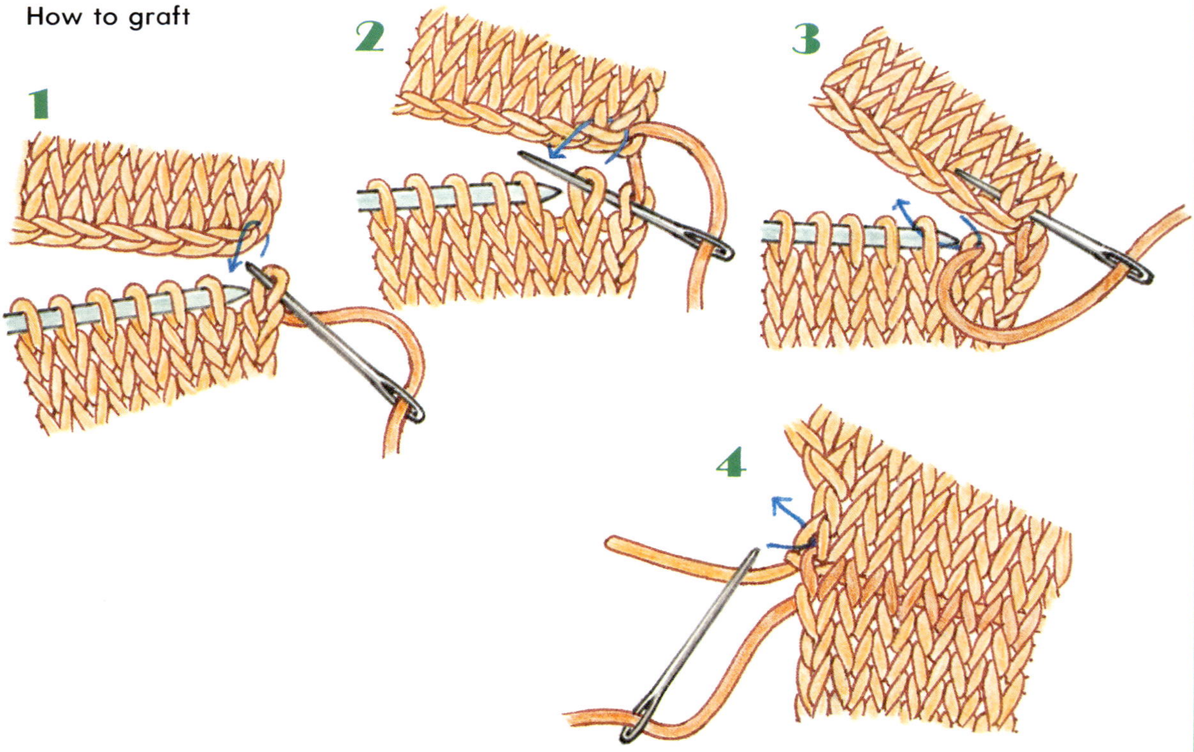

(3) Join side seams.

Place front and back, side by side, with right side up. Join side seams with remaining yarn used for casting on. Pass threaded needle through stitches on the second row from each side of front and back. Join yarn on wrong side when necessary.

(4) Join underarm seams.

Start to join seams from rib of sleeve edge. Insert needle into the stitch next to the increased st.

Invisible seams

How to join side seam of rib (A)

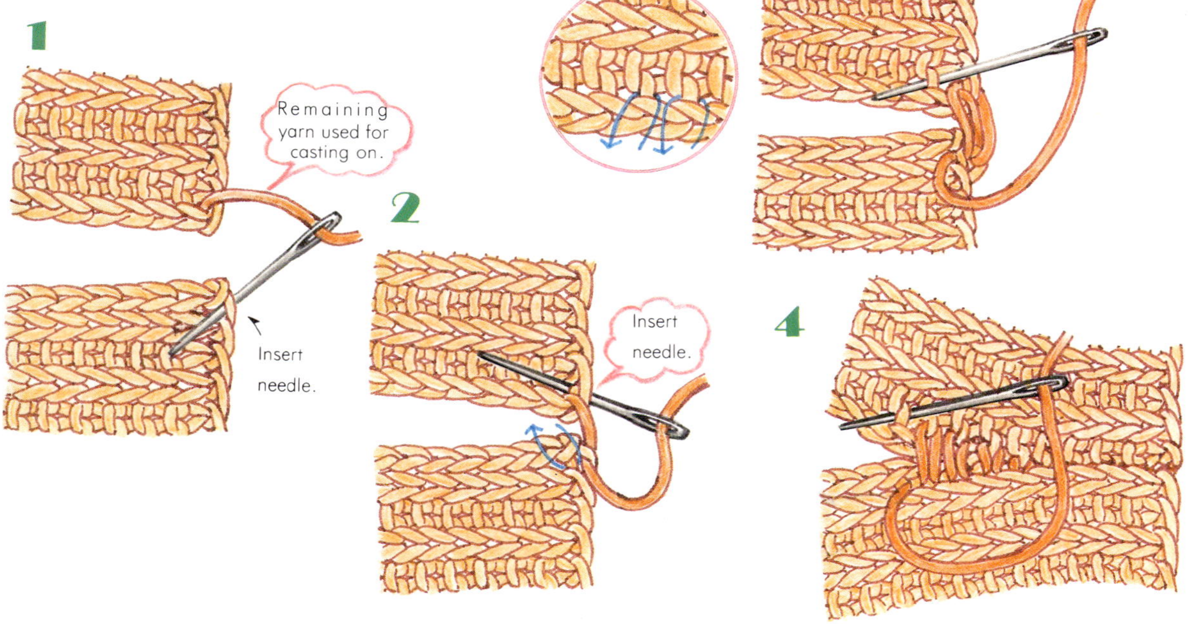

1 Remaining yarn used for casting on. Insert needle.

2 Insert needle.

3

4

How to join side seam of stockinette st.

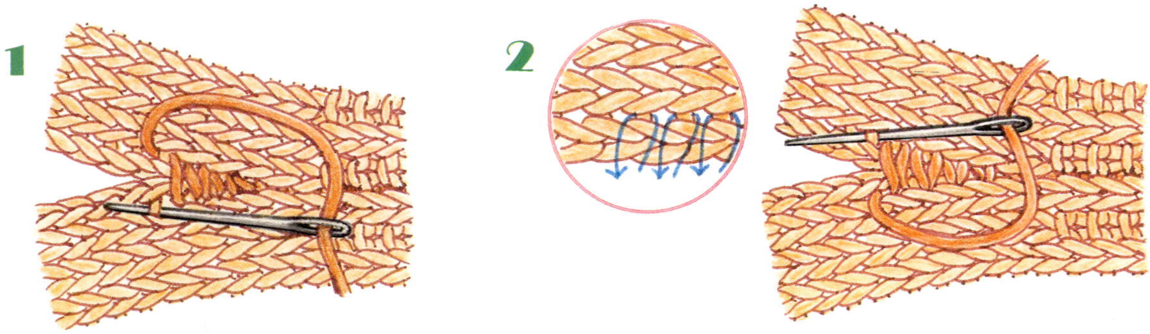

1

2

(5) Neckband.

Pick up 88 sts from neck edge with No.7 needle and divide into three groups. Work in K1, P1 rib for 8 rounds.

Number of sts to pick up

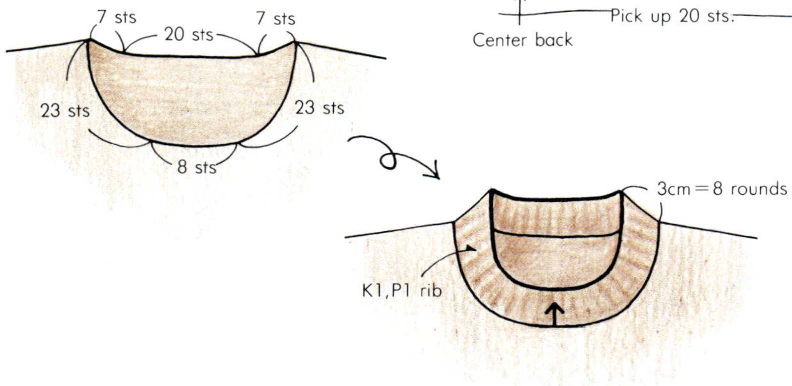

7 sts 20 sts 7 sts
23 sts 23 sts
8 sts

3cm = 8 rounds
K1, P1 rib

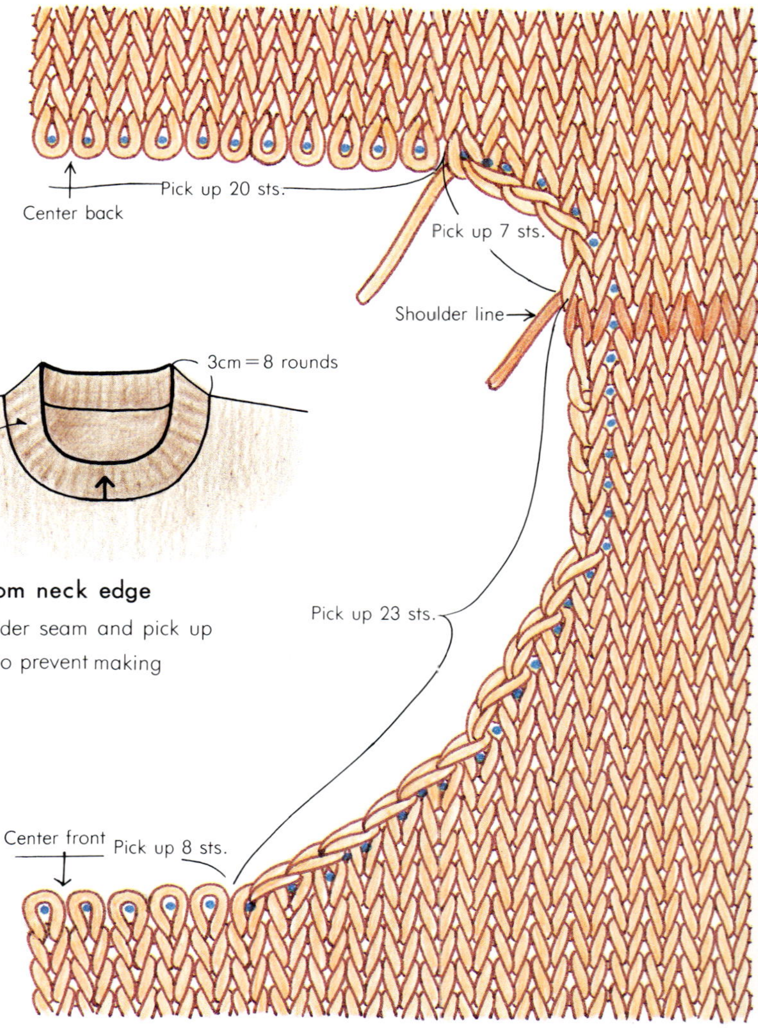

How to pick up sts from neck edge

Pick up sts starting at left shoulder seam and pick up more sts along curve as shown to prevent making holes.

Pick up 20 sts.
Center back
Pick up 7 sts.
Shoulder line
Pick up 23 sts.
Center front Pick up 8 sts.

How to fasten off in K1, P1 rib (using circular needle) See page 31 for using straight needles.

1 Insert needle into second st. End of rib. First st.
2 First st.
3
4 Repeat steps 2 and 3.
5 First st
6 Insert needle into second st. Last st of rib.
7 End of fastening off.
8 Weave end of yarn into sts of wrong side.

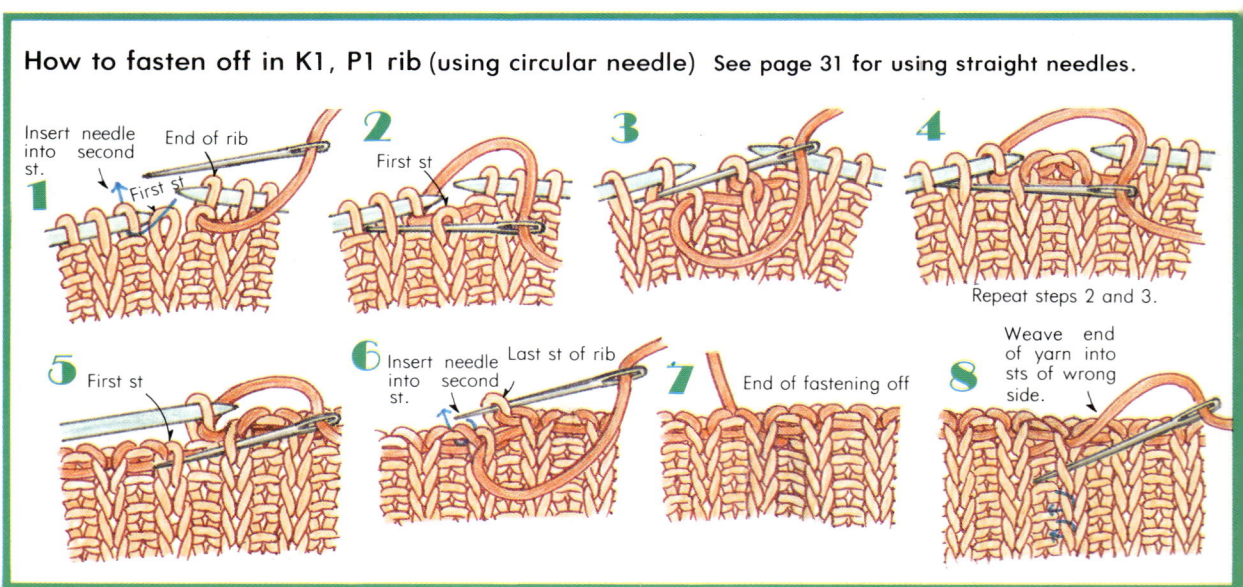

(6) Set sleeves in.

Pin sleeve and body together. Work a crocheted slip stitch along the seam line. This part needs great care, so take time and check whether sleeve fits in armhole well before fixing. Sleeves must be set in securely, but don't draw yarn too tight. For a neater finish and also to keep better shoulder line, sometimes single crochet and chain sts are worked over seams of sleeve cap after setting in sleeves. Steam-press lightly.

Crocheted slip stitch along the seam line.

How to pin sleeve and body

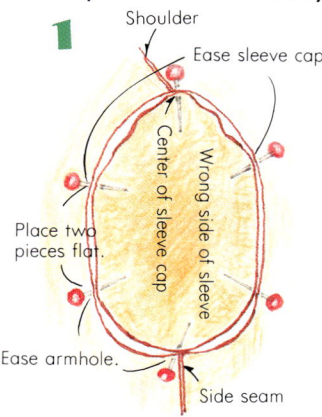

1. Shoulder / Ease sleeve cap. / Center of sleeve cap / Wrong side of sleeve / Place two pieces flat. / Ease armhole. / Side seam

Insert sleeve into armhole of body with right sides facing and pin.

2. Wrong side of sleeve

Pin more to ease fullness evenly.

Repeat inserting needle through sts every row twice and every other row once.

Crocheted slip stitch every row

Start working a crocheted slip stitch counter-clockwise from side seam. # Insert needle through stitches every row from beginning to the end of curve, then repeat inserting needle through sts every row twice and every other row once until the end of curve of back sleeve. Repeat # again and fasten off.

Crocheted slip stitch

Use this stitch for joining two pieces securely, like joining sleeves to body. With right sides facing, work a crocheted slip stitch with crochet hook.

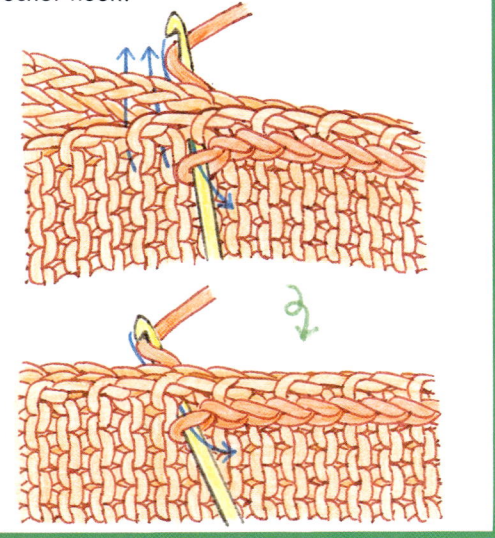

How to crochet over seams

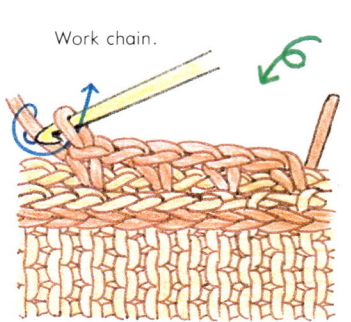
Work chain.

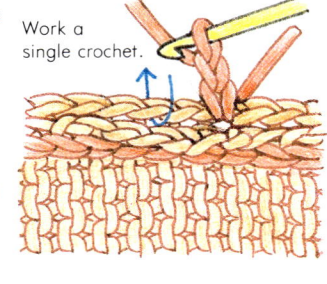
Work a single crochet.

Repeats of sc and ch are worked over seams of sleeve cap.

(7) Steam-press all over the finished sweater.

Prepare the followings.

MATERIALS: Bulky yarn (100% wool, 2oz.=123yds): navy, 460g; off-white, 200g; red, 20g.
EQUIPMENT: Knitting needles: No. 5 (3.9mm) one set each of two and four; No. 7 (4.5mm) one set of two. Crochet hook size 4/E (3.5mm). Tapestry needle. Stitch holders. Markers.

Finished size

GAUGE

21 sts = 10cm; 25 rows = 10cm in seed and stockinette sts.

Raglan-sleeved sweaters are always comfortable and practical. How about knitting your own sweater reversing colors of top and bottom to match his?

Back

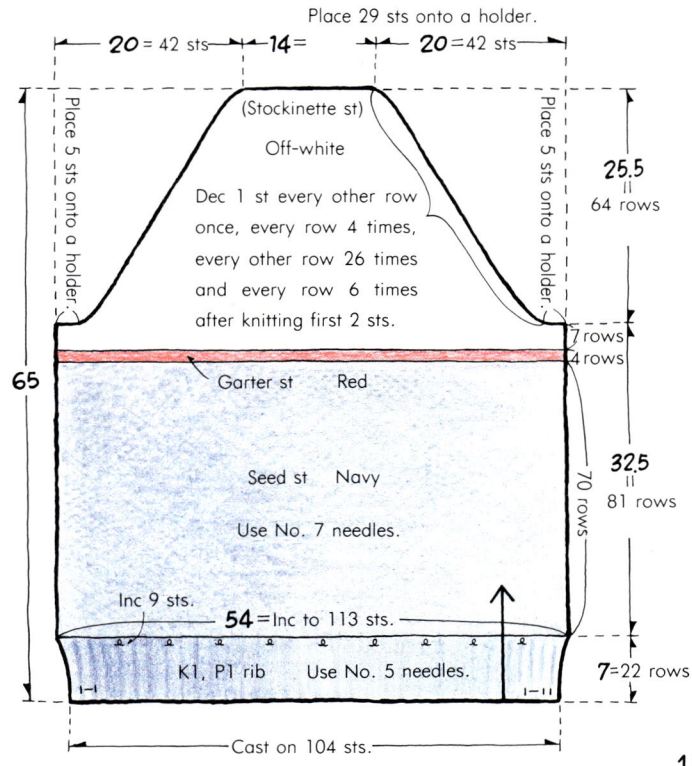

(1) Cast on 104 sts.

Ch 104 with crochet hook size 4/E using contrasting yarn which is later removed. Pick up 53 sts through loops of chain with No. 5 knitting needle and yarn to be used for rib. Pick up sts through first 2 loops and then through every other loop from third one.

How to cast on sts for K1, P1 rib

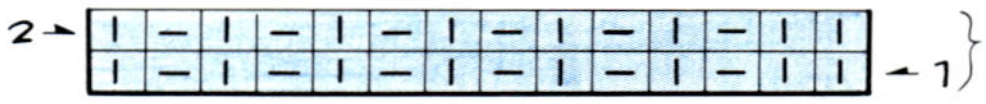

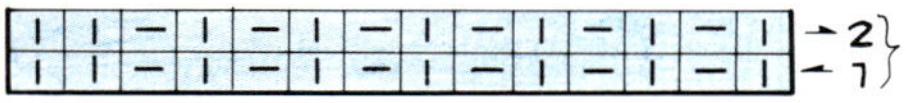

In case of making first 2 sts of right side in knit st.

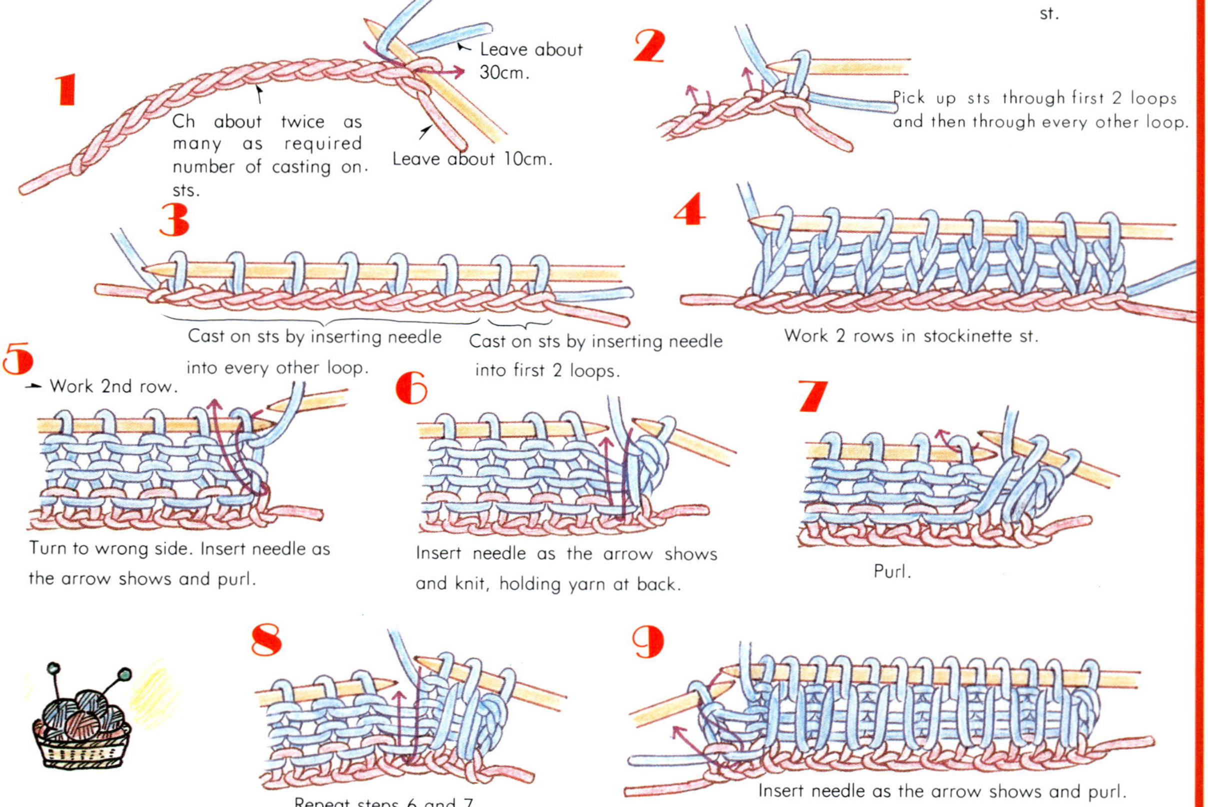

1 Ch about twice as many as required number of casting on sts. Leave about 30cm. Leave about 10cm.

2 Pick up sts through first 2 loops and then through every other loop.

3 Cast on sts by inserting needle into every other loop. Cast on sts by inserting needle into first 2 loops.

4 Work 2 rows in stockinette st.

5 Work 2nd row.

6 Turn to wrong side. Insert needle as the arrow shows and purl.

Insert needle as the arrow shows and knit, holding yarn at back.

7 Purl.

8 Repeat steps 6 and 7.

9 Insert needle as the arrow shows and purl.

In case of making last 2 sts on left side in knit st.

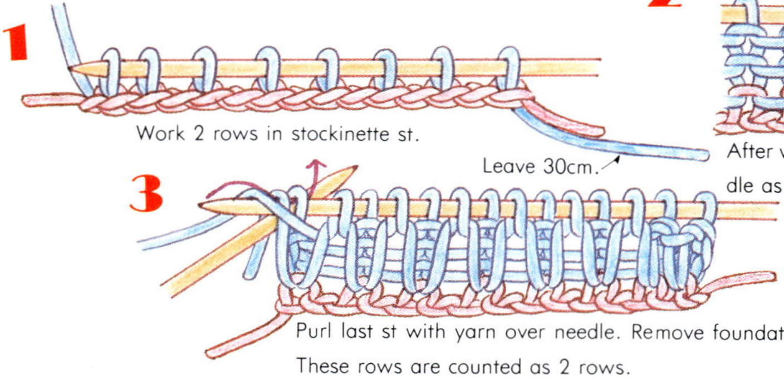

1 Work 2 rows in stockinette st. Leave 30cm.

2 Turn to wrong side and work 2nd row. Knit. Purl. After working 2nd row, insert right needle as the arrow shows and purl.

3 Purl last st with yarn over needle. Remove foundation chain. These rows are counted as 2 rows.

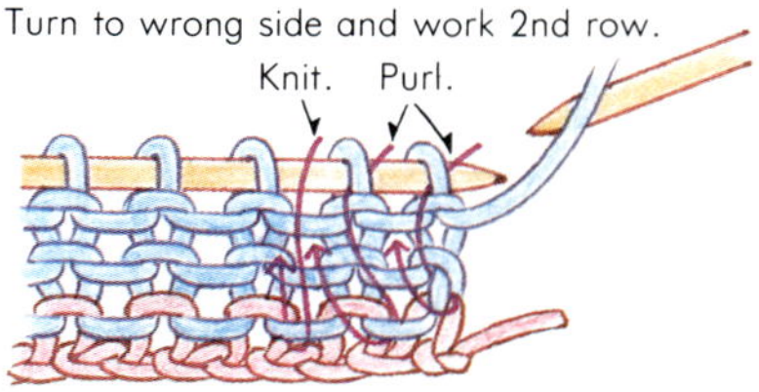

(2) Work in K1, P1 rib.

Two rows have been made when casting on, so continue to work in K1, P1 rib from third row to 21st row. Work in reverse st st on 22nd row, increasing 9 sts evenly spaced.

See page 12 for increasing.

(3) Work even for 81 rows.

Change to No. 7 needles and work even for 70 rows in seed st. Change to red and work for 4 rows in garter st, and then change to white and work for 7 rows in st st.

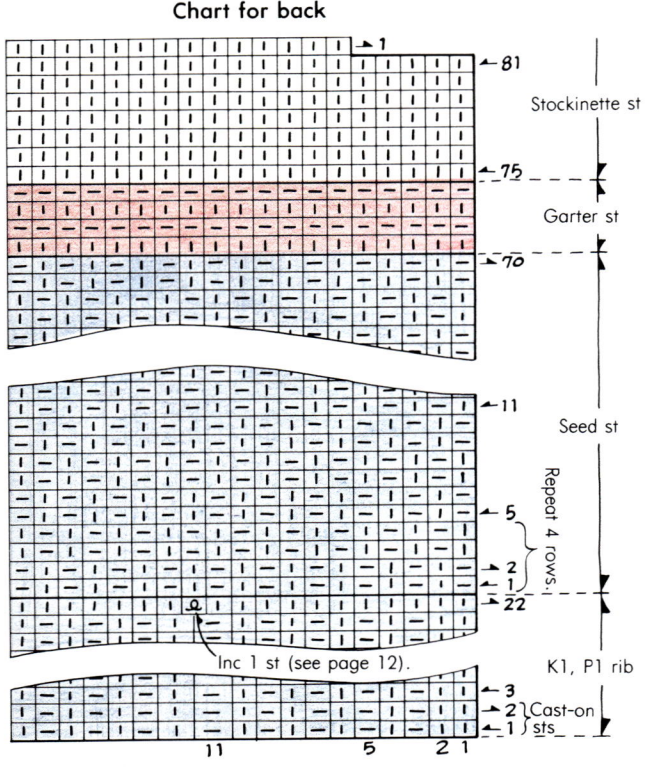

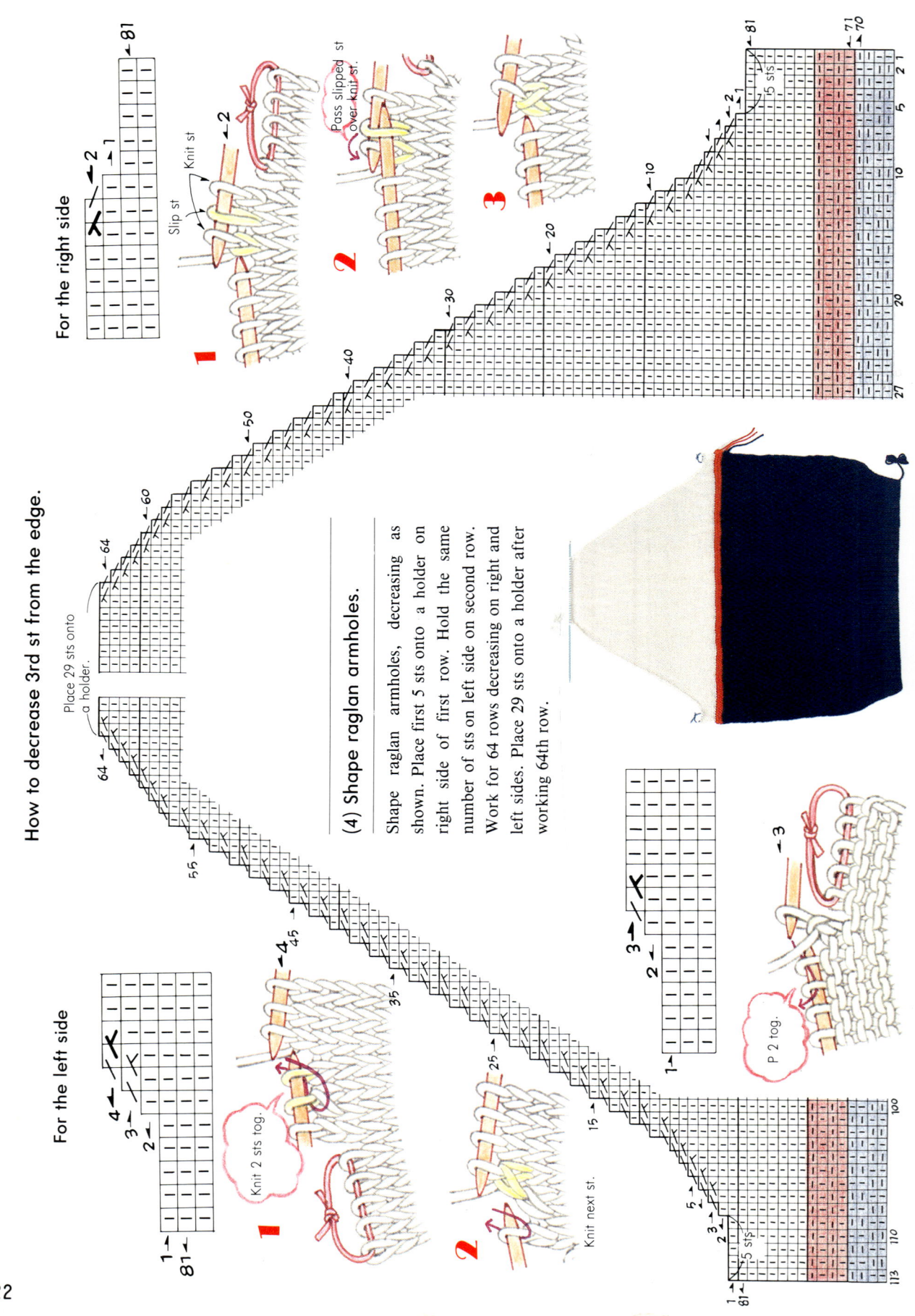

Front

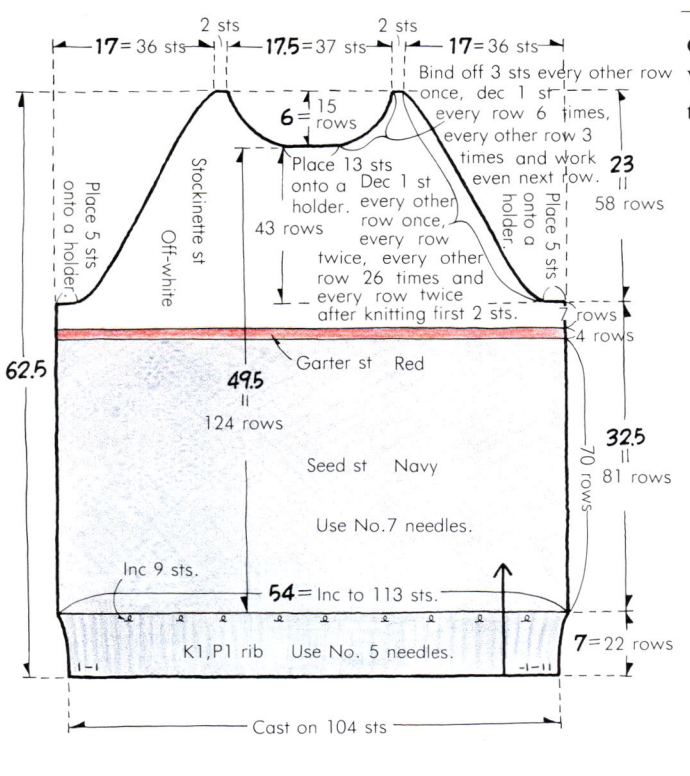

(1) Cast on 104 sts and work to the neck edge.

Cast on 104 sts and work to 81st row as for back. Work to 43rd row decreasing on right and left sides to shape raglan armholes.

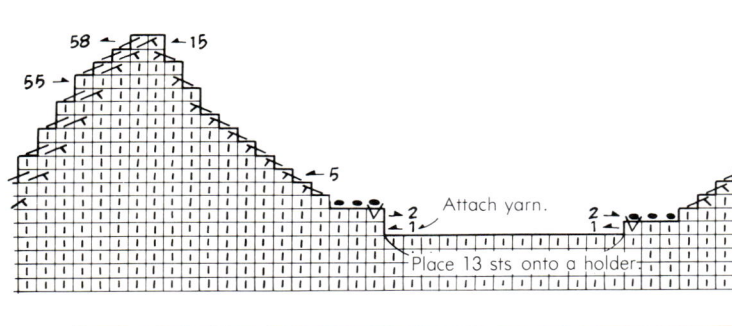

(2) Shape neck.

Work for right side first. After working right side of 44th row (first row of neck edge), place 13 sts at center front onto a holder and hold remaining sts on knitting needle for left shoulder. Work to 15th row to shape neck and place last 2 sts onto a safety pin. Work for left side in same manner.

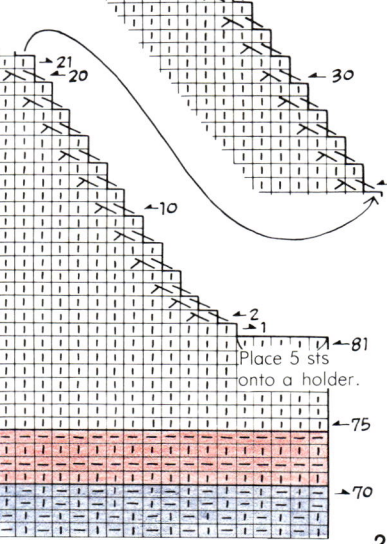

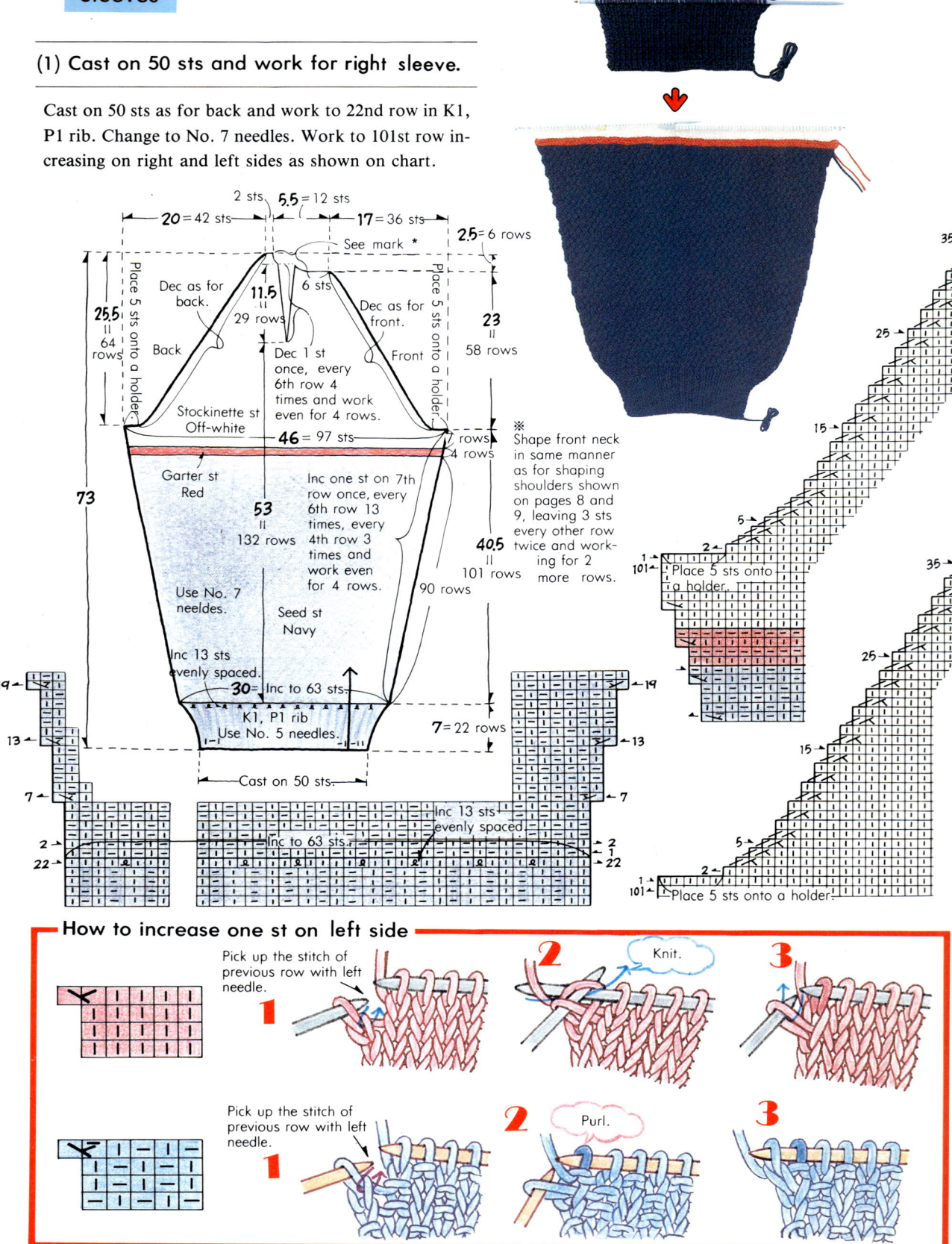

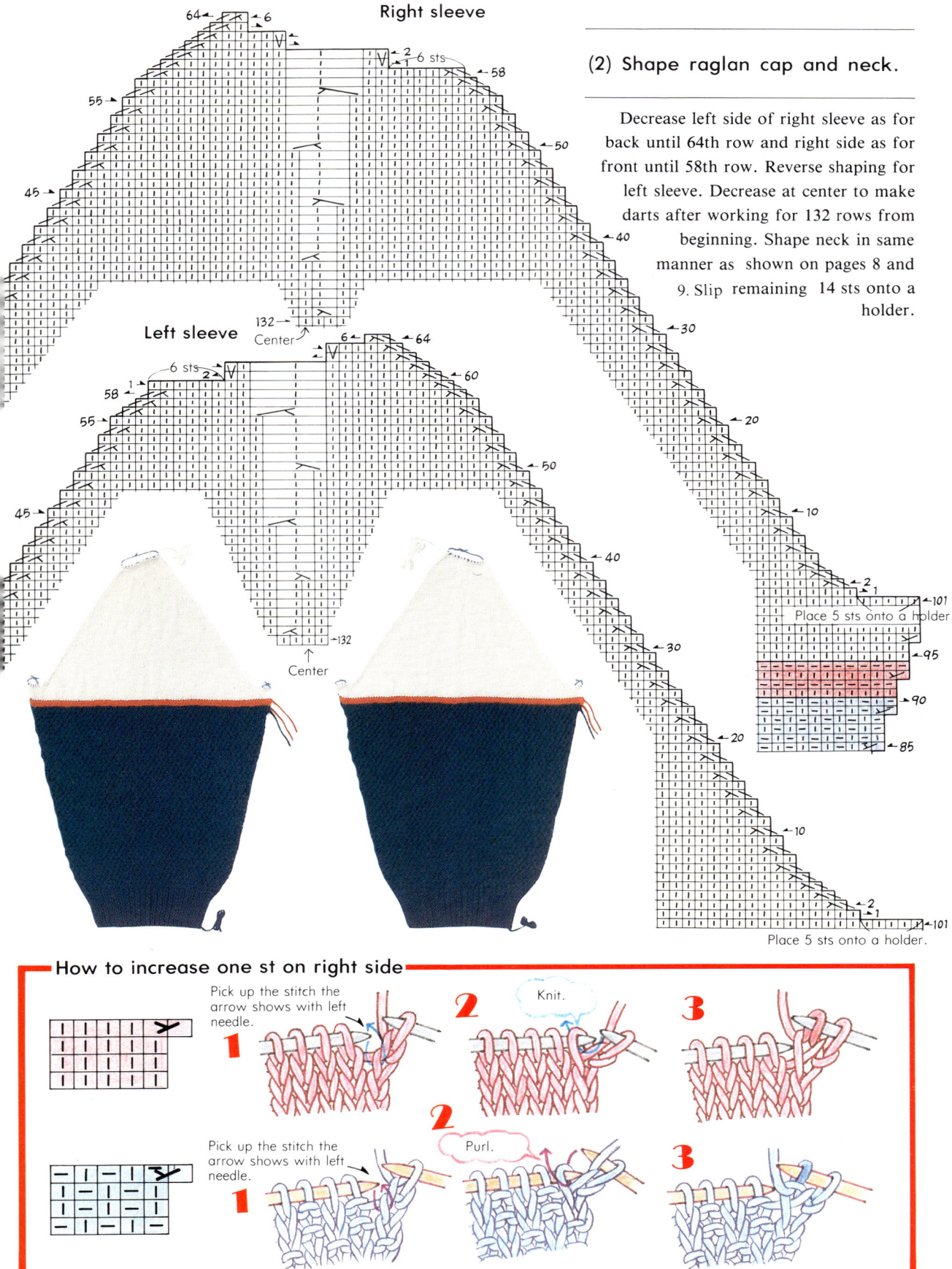

Finishing

(2) Join raglan sleeves and body pieces.

(1) Block with steam iron.

Block knit pieces with steam iron before joining.

How to join raglan sleeve and front (or back)

Place front (or back) and sleeve with right sides facing. Work a crocheted slip stitch to join 5 sts each of front (or back) and sleeve. Turn to right side. Using tapestry needle join front (or back) and sleeve along seam line.

1 Work a crocheted slip stitch to join 5 sts.

2 Draw yarn through last chain.

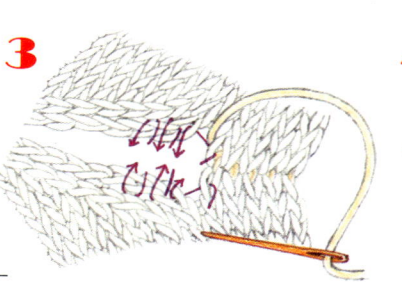

3 Turn to right side and join with tapestry needle.

4

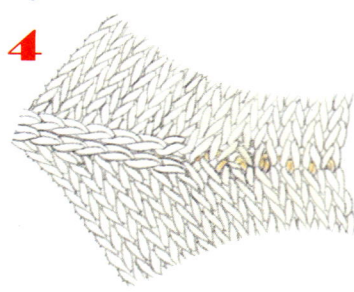

(3) Join side and sleeve seams.

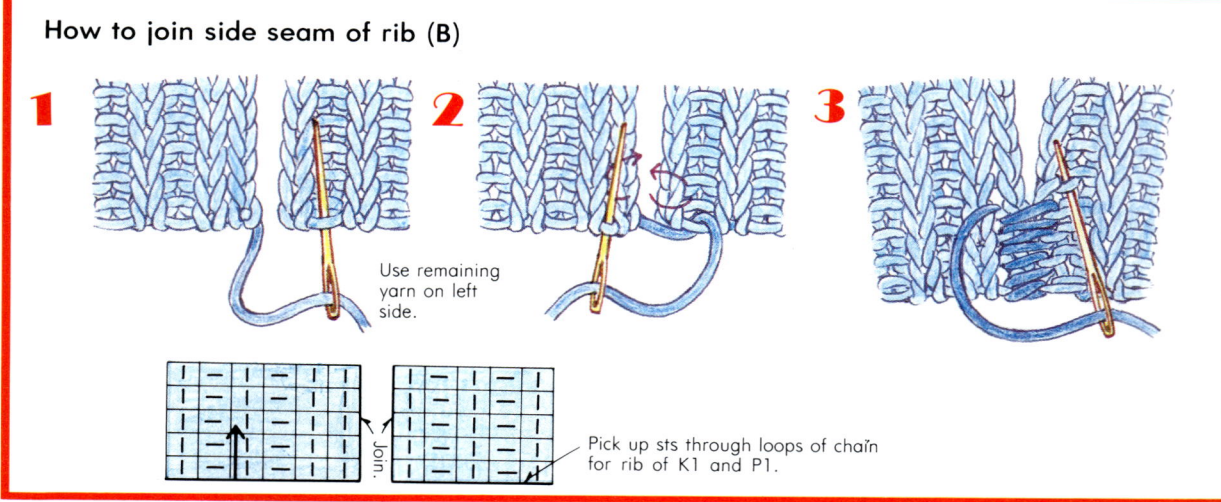

How to join side seam of rib (B)

1 Use remaining yarn on left side.

2

3

Pick up sts through loops of chain for rib of K1 and P1.

(4) Neckband and finishing.

Change to No. 5 needles. Pick up 96 sts starting at left sleeve. Work for 10 rounds. Bind off loosely in rib (see page 16). Block finished sweater with steam iron.

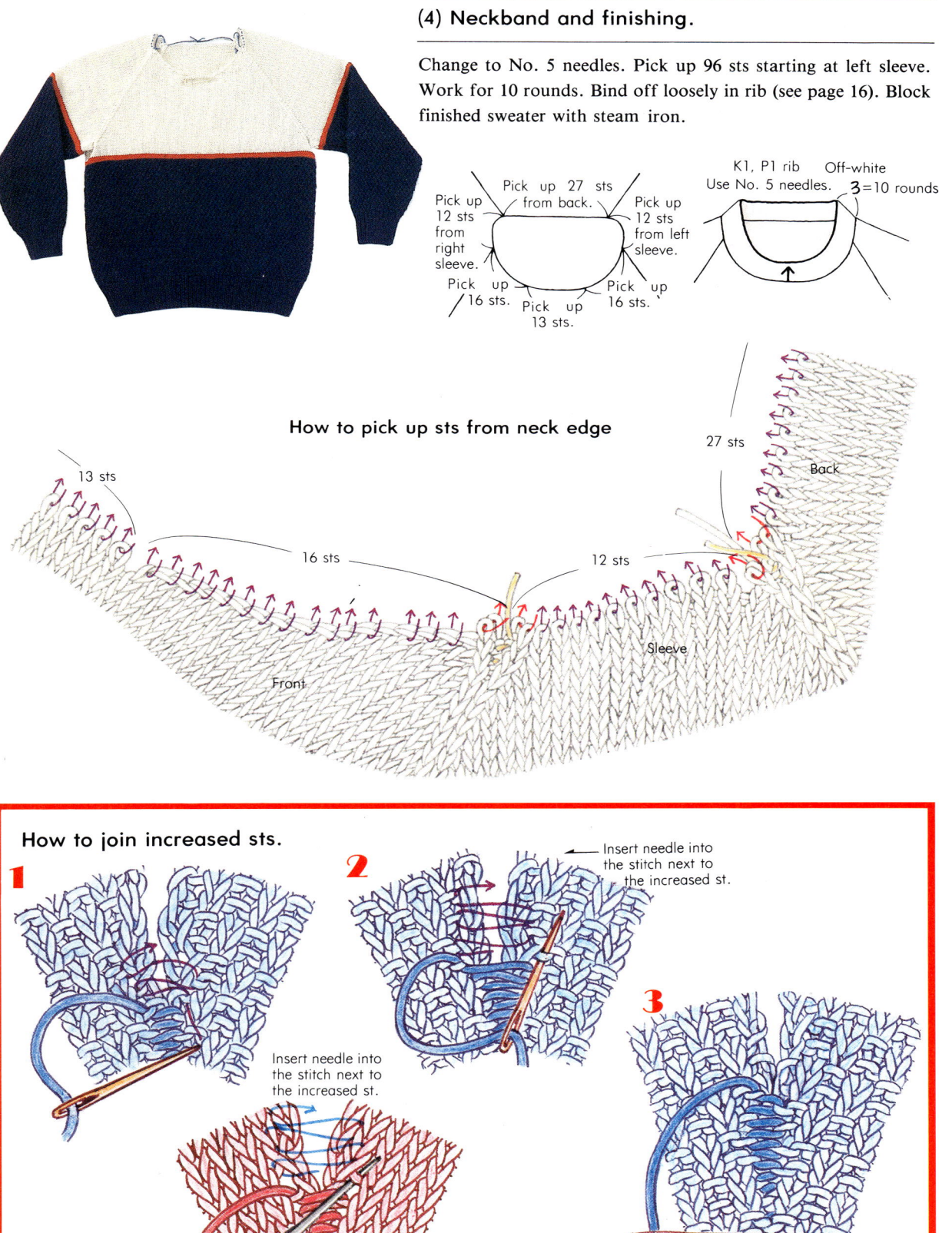

ARGYLE VEST

Prepare the followings.

MATERIALS: Bulky yarn (100% wool, 2oz.=123yds): gray, 290g charcoal gray, 40g; blue, 40g.
EQUIPMENT: Knitting needles: No. 5 (3.9mm), one set each of two and four; No. 7 (4.5mm) one set of two. Crochet hook size 4/E (3.5mm). Tapestry needle. Stitch holders. Markers.

Finished size

46cm
65.5cm
98cm

For vest in one color

Use one color and work as for Argyle Vest.

Red
Powder green   320g each
Brown

GAUGE

19 sts = 10cm; 23 rows = 10cm in stockinette st and pattern st.

This argyle vest goes well with any jacket and shirt. You can make the vest with one color as shown on opposite page.

Back

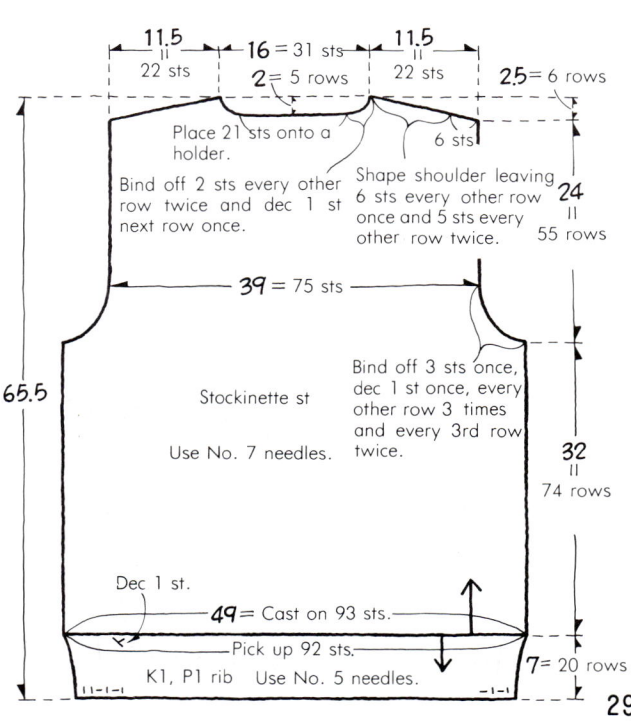

11.5 = 22 sts
16 = 31 sts
11.5 = 22 sts
2 = 5 rows
2.5 = 6 rows

Place 21 sts onto a holder.
Bind off 2 sts every other row twice and dec 1 st next row once.
Shape shoulder leaving 6 sts every other row once and 5 sts every other row twice.
6 sts
24 = 55 rows

39 = 75 sts

Stockinette st
Use No. 7 needles.

Bind off 3 sts once, dec 1 st once, every other row 3 times and every 3rd row twice.
32 = 74 rows

65.5

Dec 1 st.
49 = Cast on 93 sts.
Pick up 92 sts.
K1, P1 rib Use No. 5 needles.
7 = 20 rows

(1) Cast on 93 sts and work even to 74th row.

Use yarn easy to remove later for making chain. Ch 93 loosely with crochet hook. Pick up 93 sts through loops of chain — this is counted as first row of knit st. Remove chain later. Work even in st st to 74th row.

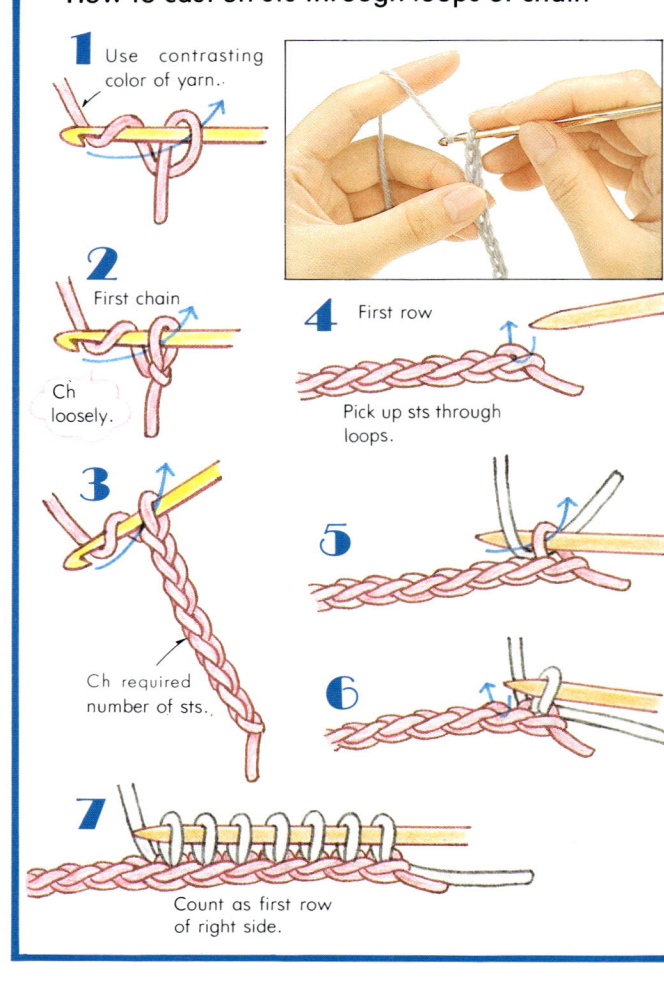

How to cast on sts through loops of chain

1. Use contrasting color of yarn.
2. First chain. Ch loosely.
3. Ch required number of sts.
4. First row. Pick up sts through loops.
5.
6.
7. Count as first row of right side.

(2) Shape armholes, shoulders and neck.

Shape shoulders in same manner as shown on pages 8 and 9 and at the same time shape neck. Hold 22 sts on each side after shaping shoulders until joining.

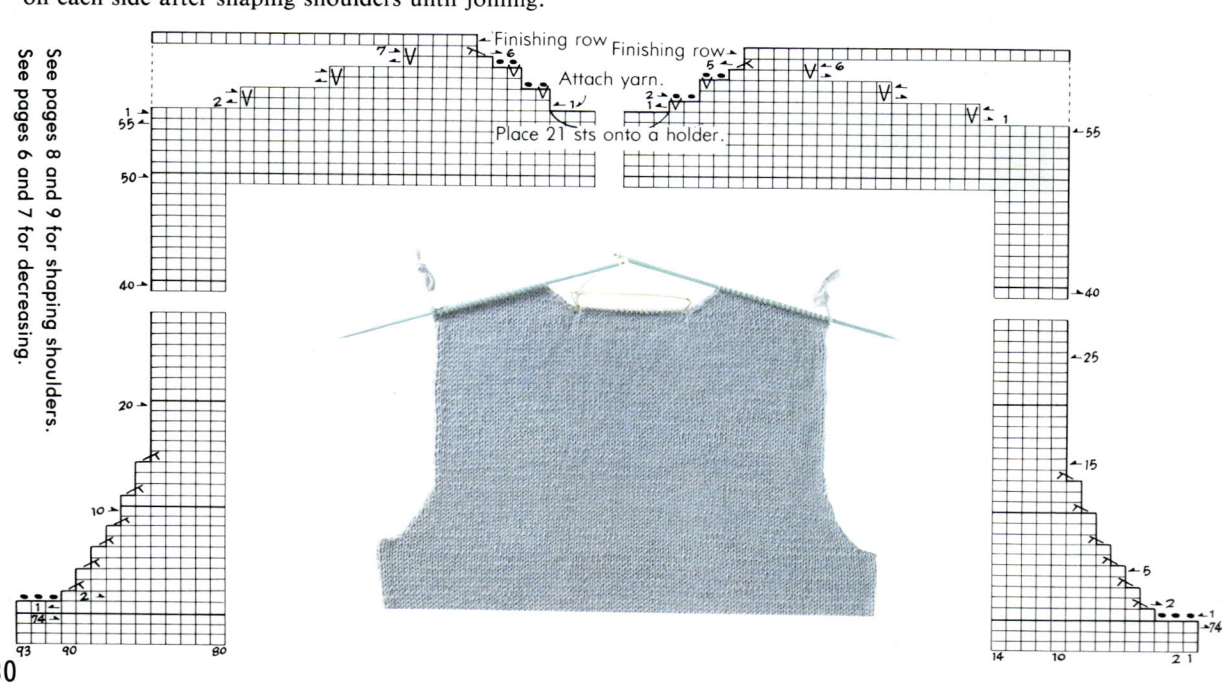

(3) Work in rib for bottomband and bind off in rib.

Change to No. 5 needles. Pick up 92 sts from bottom edge (dec 1 st) and work in K1, P1 rib to 20th row. Cut off yarn leaving about 150cm. Bind off in rib. Remove chain.

Chart for K1, P1 rib

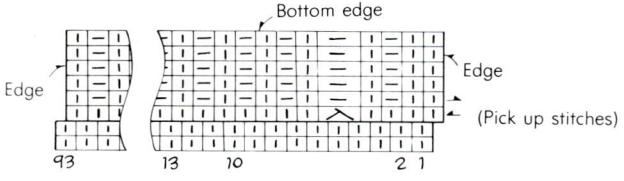

How to pick up sts from the starting edge

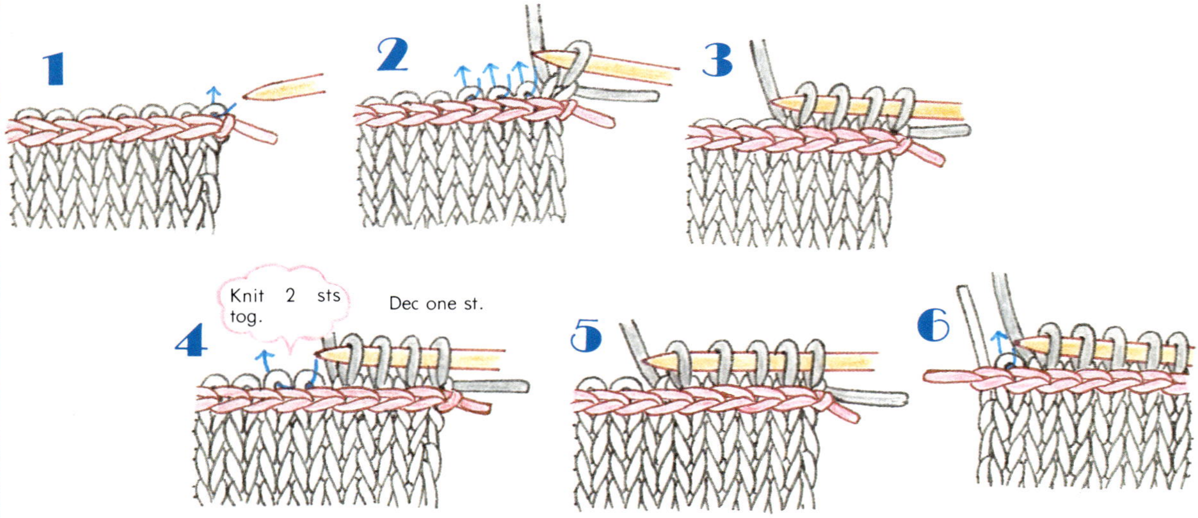

1
2
3
4 — Knit 2 sts tog. Dec one st.
5
6

How to fasten off in K1, P1 rib (using straight needles)

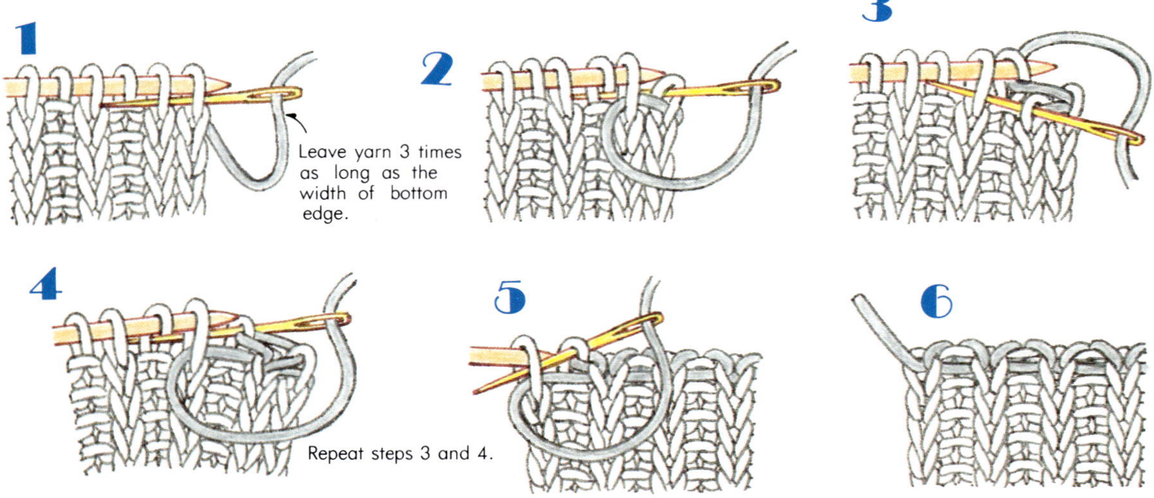

1 — Leave yarn 3 times as long as the width of bottom edge.
2
3
4
5 — Repeat steps 3 and 4.
6

31

Front

(1) Cast on 93 sts.

Ch 93 loosely with contrasting color and pick up 93 sts with No. 7 needle and gray yarn through loops of chain as for back.

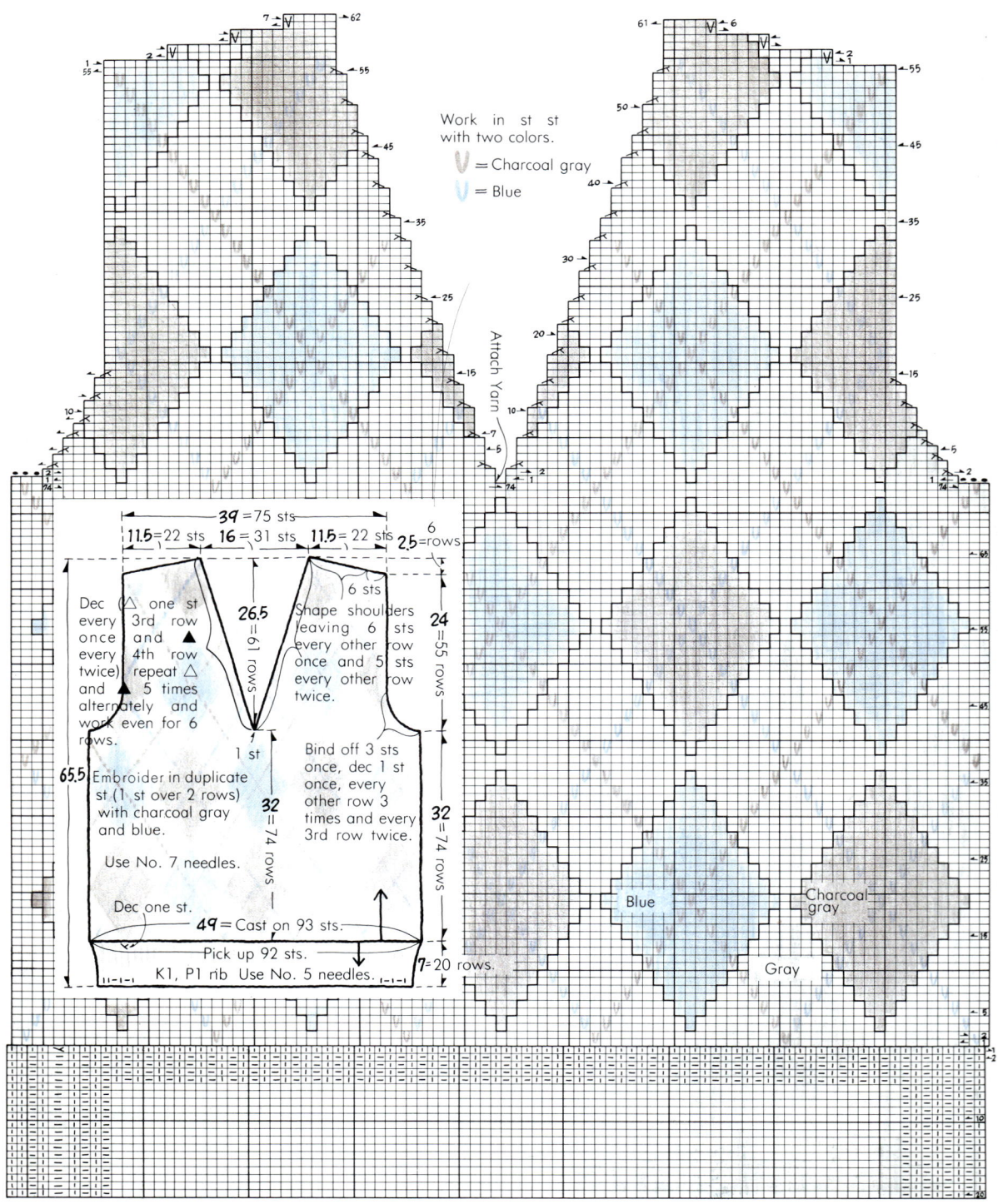

(2) Work even in st st to 74th row.

Work 2nd row with gray, then work even to 74th row in st st changing colors as shown on chart.

How to change colors
(by attaching yarn for each motif)

Attach yarn for each motif and knit twisting yarns as shown below.

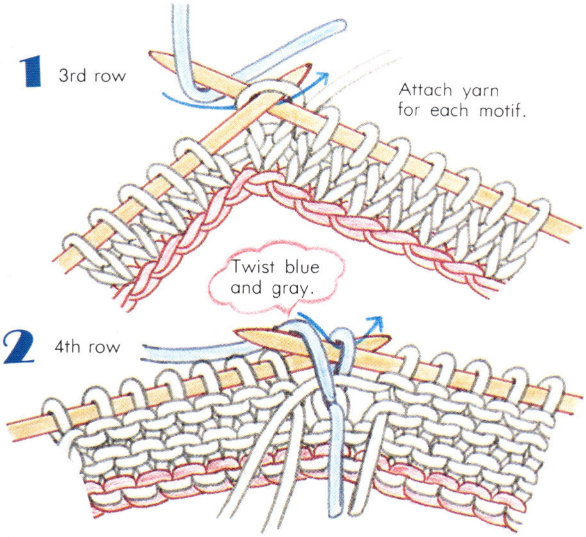

1 3rd row Attach yarn for each motif.

Twist blue and gray.

2 4th row

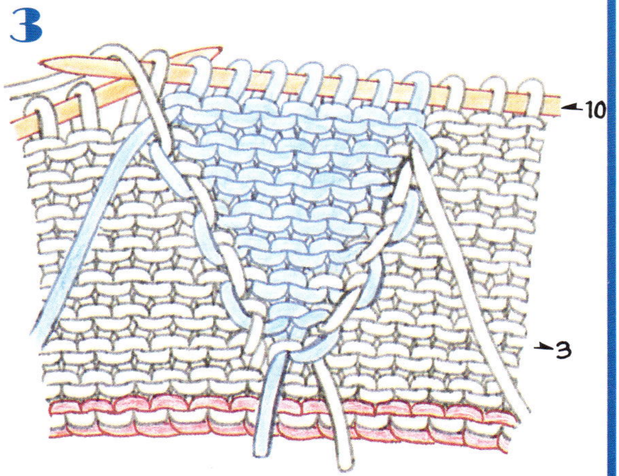

3 ←10 ←3

Wrong side

Weave ends of yarn into sts on wrong side.

Attach yarn for each motif.

(3) Shape armholes and neck.

Work for right side (left shoulder) first. Bind off 3 sts and knit to center of the row. Hold one st at center and place remaining 46 sts onto another needle. Shape armholes and neck decreasing as shown on chart of page 32. After working until 55th row, shape shoulder in same manner as shown on pages 8 and 9. Hold 22 sts without working finishing row. Attach yarn at neck edge to make left side (right shoulder). Shape neck reversing right side but start to shape armhole and shoulder one row behind the right side.

How to make V-neck

How to decrease for left side

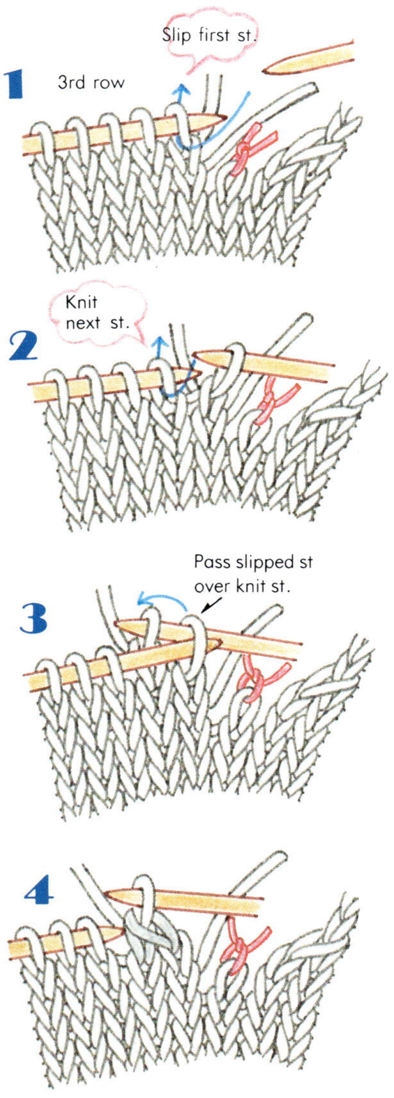

1. 3rd row — Slip first st.
2. Knit next st.
3. Pass slipped st over knit st.
4.

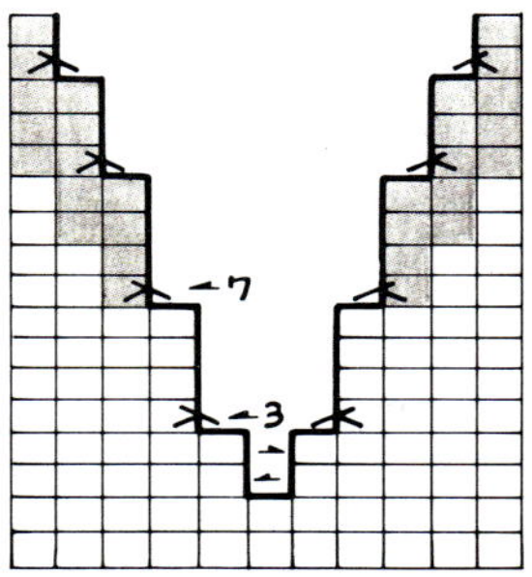

How to decrease for right side

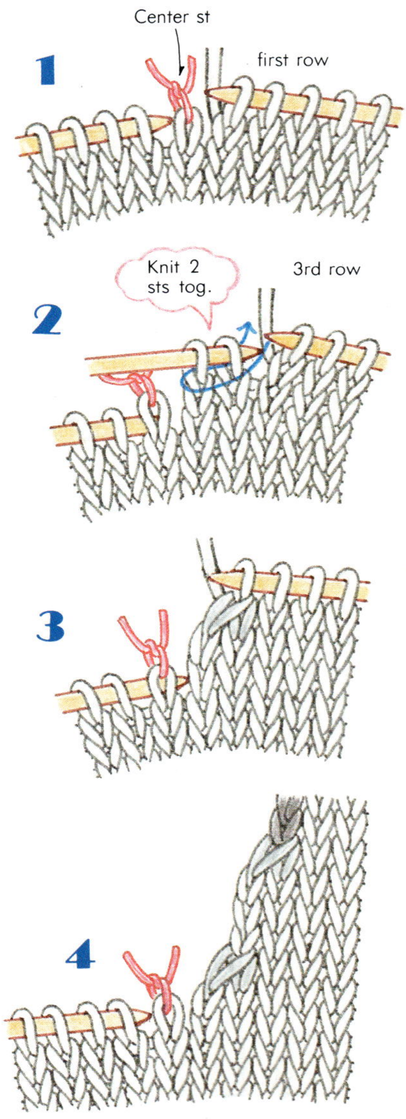

1. Center st — first row
2. 3rd row — Knit 2 sts tog.
3.
4.

Embroider in duplicate st (1 st over 2 rows)

1
2
3

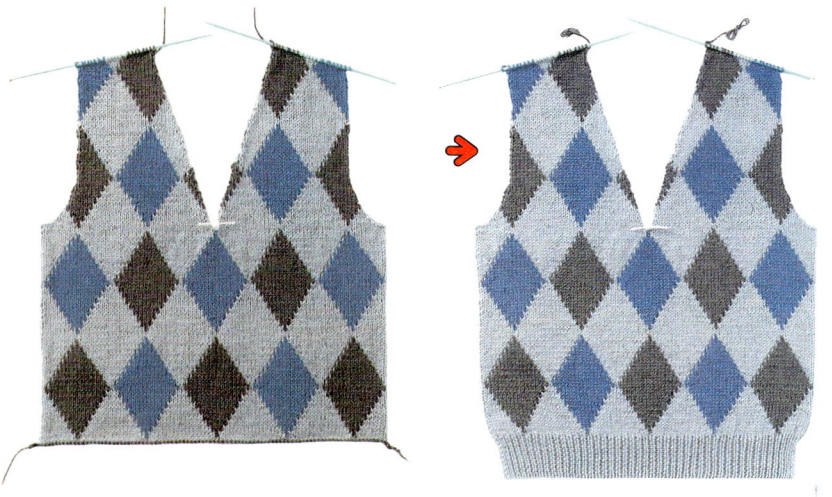

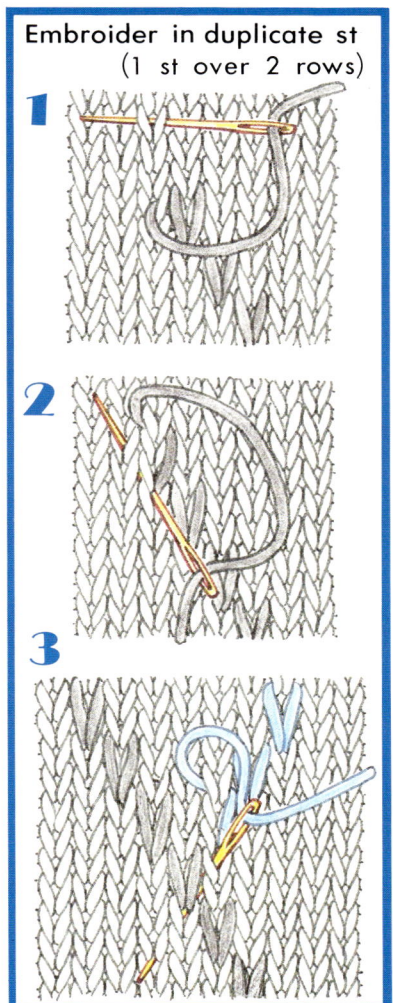

(4) Bottomband.

Pick up 92 sts from bottom edge with No. 5 needle. Work in K1, P1 rib to 20th row and bind off loosely in rib.

(5) Embroider in duplicate st (1 st over 2 rows).

Steam-press and embroider diagonally as shown at right.

Finishing

(1) Join shoulder seams.

Steam-press front and back. With right sides facing, join shoulder seams as shown below.

How to work a crocheted slip stitch.

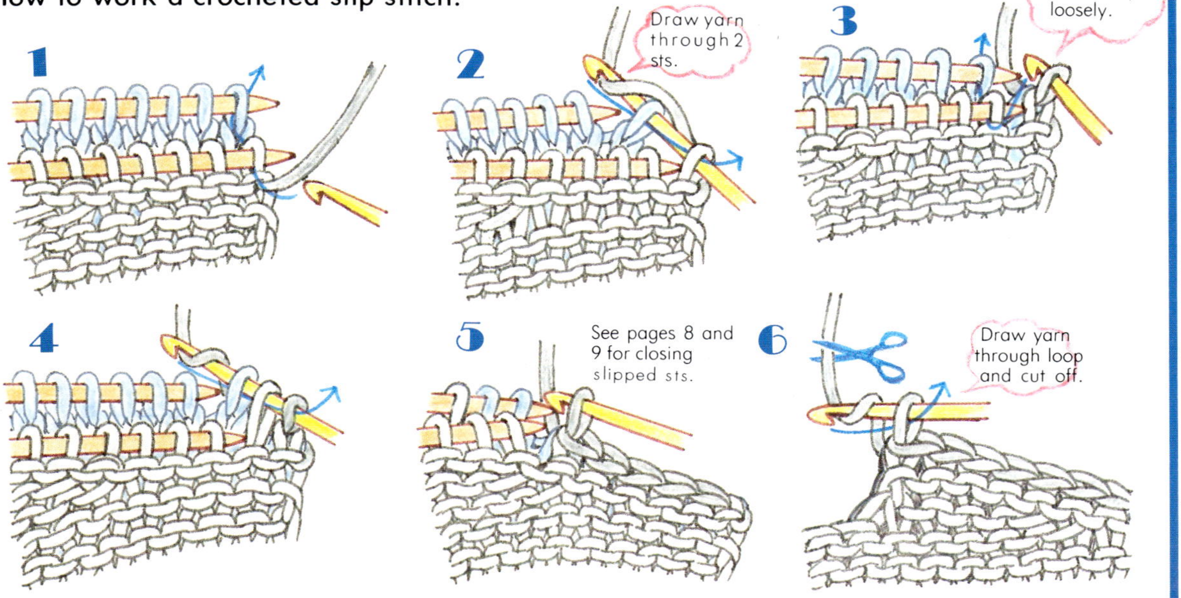

1
2
Draw yarn through 2 sts.
3
Make loop loosely.
4
5
See pages 8 and 9 for closing slipped sts.
6
Draw yarn through loop and cut off.

(2) Join side seams.

Join side seams with right sides facing.

How to join side seam of rib (C)

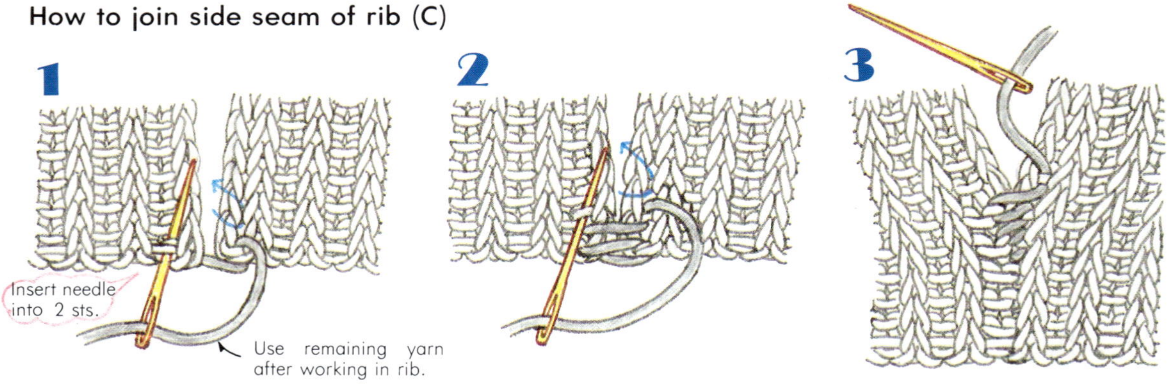

1 Insert needle into 2 sts. Use remaining yarn after working in rib.

2

3

In case of beginning and ending K1.

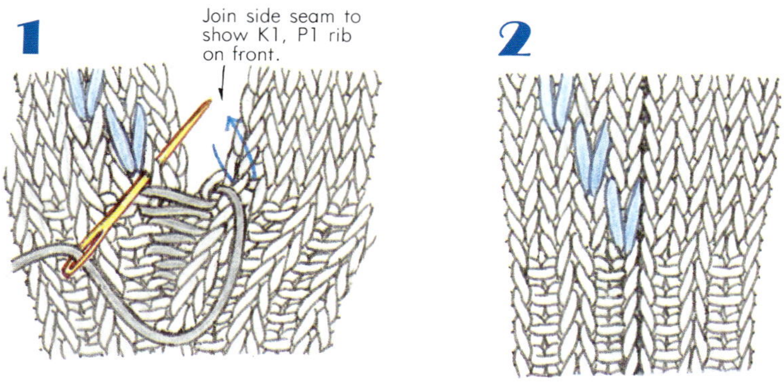

1 Join side seam to show K1, P1 rib on front.

2

How to pick up sts from armhole

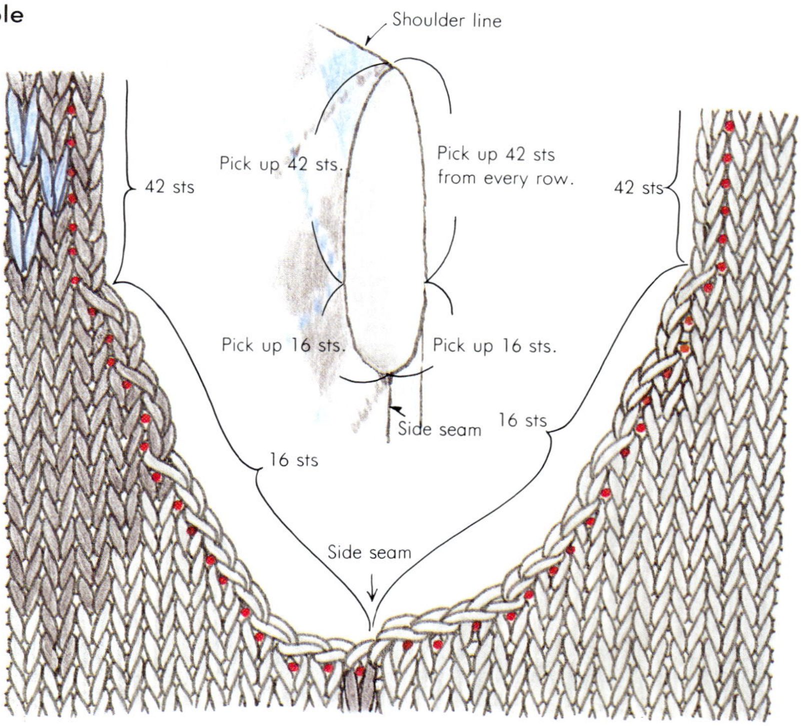

Shoulder line

Pick up 42 sts. — 42 sts

Pick up 42 sts from every row. — 42 sts

Pick up 16 sts.

Pick up 16 sts.

16 sts

Side seam

16 sts

Side seam

(3) Neckband and armbands.

Pick up 166 sts around neck edge, starting at left shoulder seam. Divide into 3 groups and work in K1, P1 rib decreasing 2 sts at center neck as shown below. Then work for armbands. Pick up 116 sts around armhole starting at side seam. Work in K1, P1 rib for 10 rounds and bind off in rib.

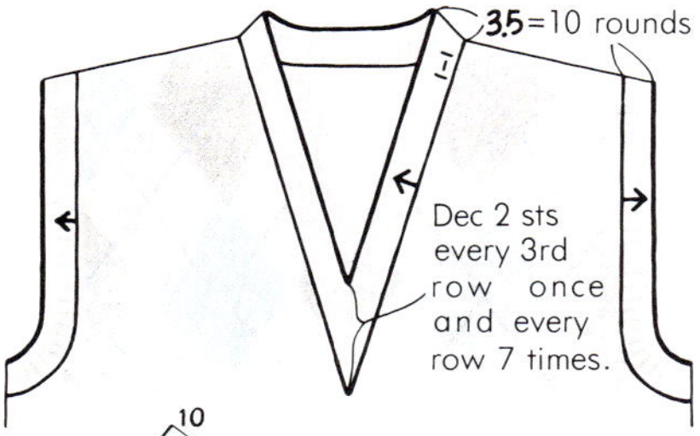

3.5=10 rounds
1-1
Dec 2 sts every 3rd row once and every row 7 times.

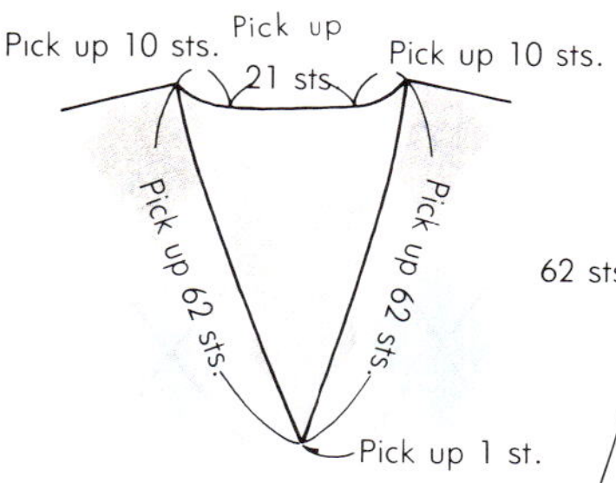

Pick up 10 sts.
Pick up 21 sts
Pick up 10 sts.
Pick up 62 sts.
Pick up 62 sts.
Pick up 1 st.

How to pick up sts around neck edge.

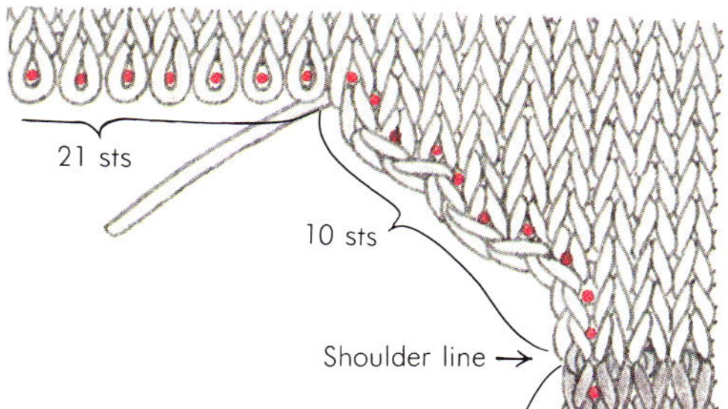
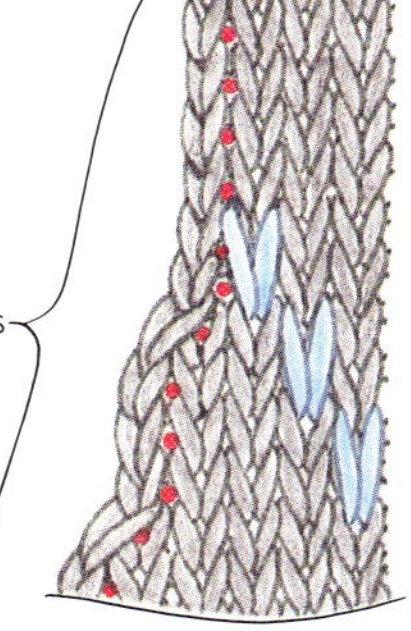
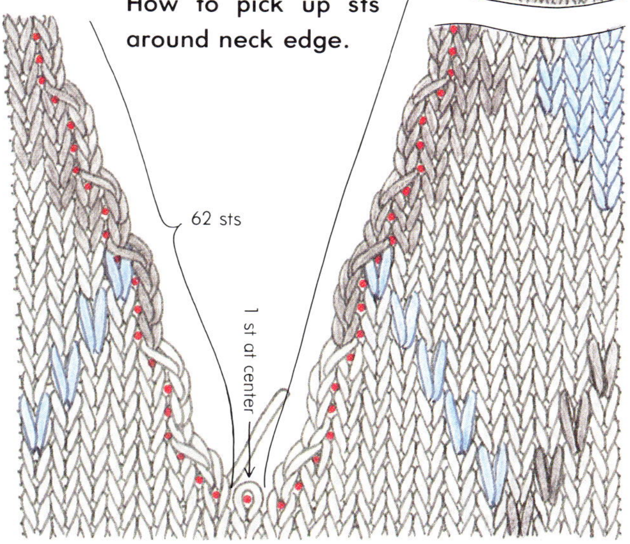

21 sts
10 sts
Shoulder line
62 sts
62 sts
1 st at center

Chart for center neck

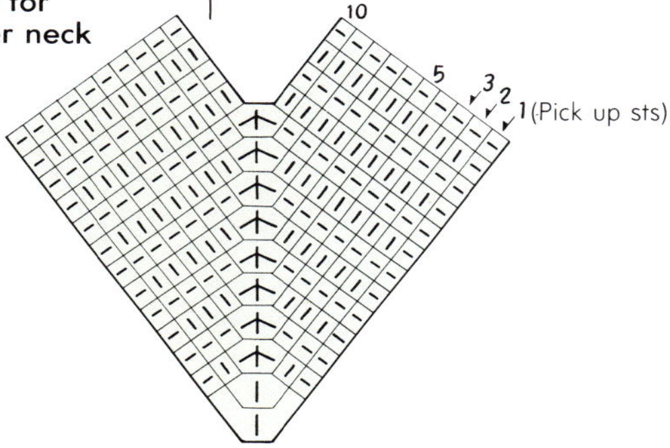

10
5
3
2
1(Pick up sts)

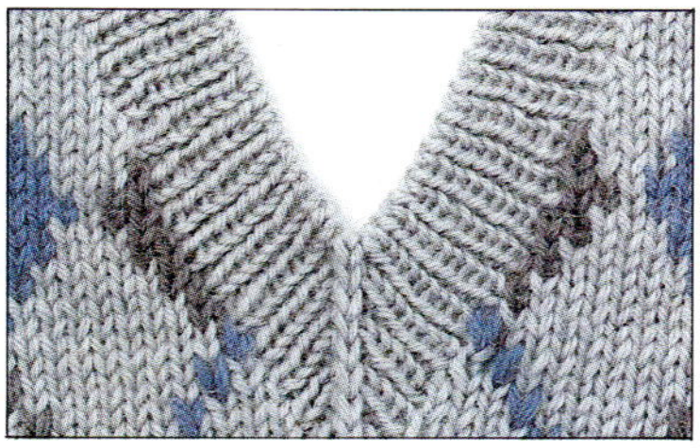

How to dec 2 sts at center (in K1, P1 rib)

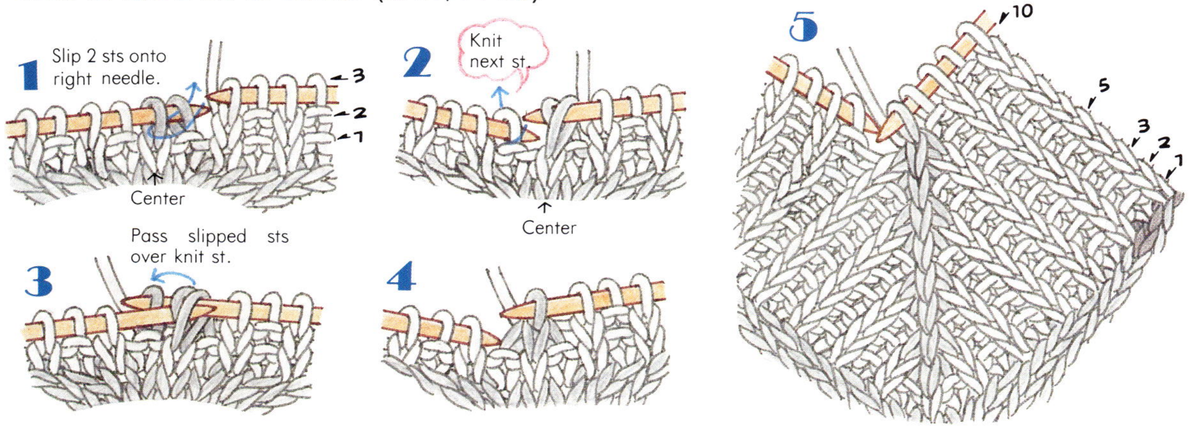

1
Slip 2 sts onto right needle.
3
2
1
Center
2
Knit next st.
Center
3
Pass slipped sts over knit st.
4
5
10
5
3
2
1

(4) Finishing.

Steam-press lightly.

HENLY NECK SWEATER

Prepare the followings.

MATERIALS: Bulky yarn (100% wool, 2oz.=98yds): off-white, 740g.
EQUIPMENT: Knitting needles: No. 5 (3.9mm) one set each of two and four; No. 7 (4.5mm) one set of two. Crochet hook size 4/E (3.5mm). Tapestry needle. 2 buttons, 2cm in diameter. 2 small buttons. Stitch holders. Markers.

GAUGE
19 sts = 10cm; 24 rows = 10cm in pattern st.

Back

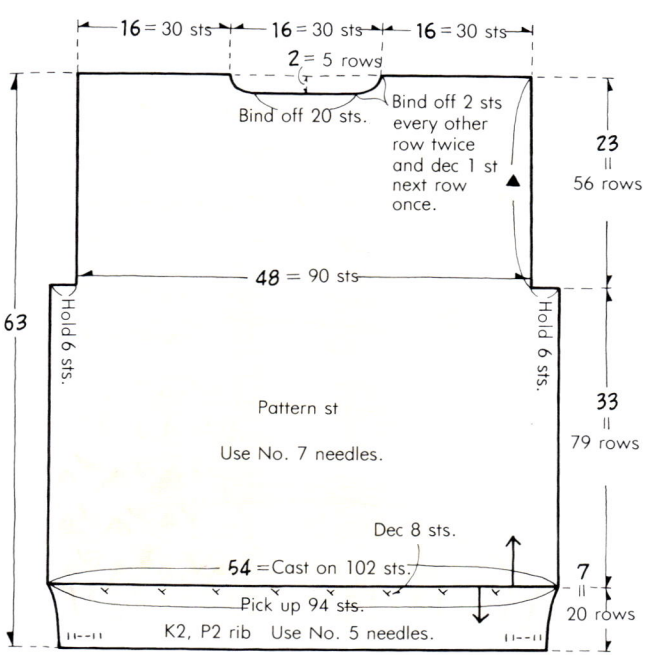

Finished size

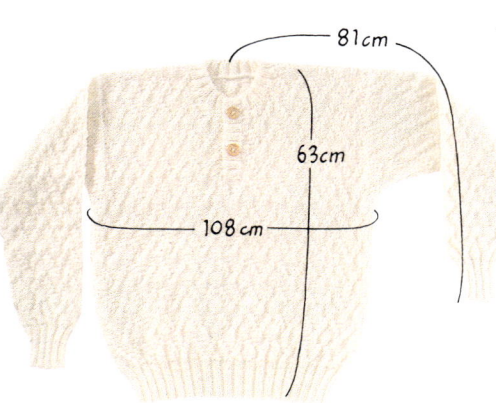

This beautiful sweater is knitted in all-over chevron pattern. It looks difficult to make but is truly easy.

Chart for pattern

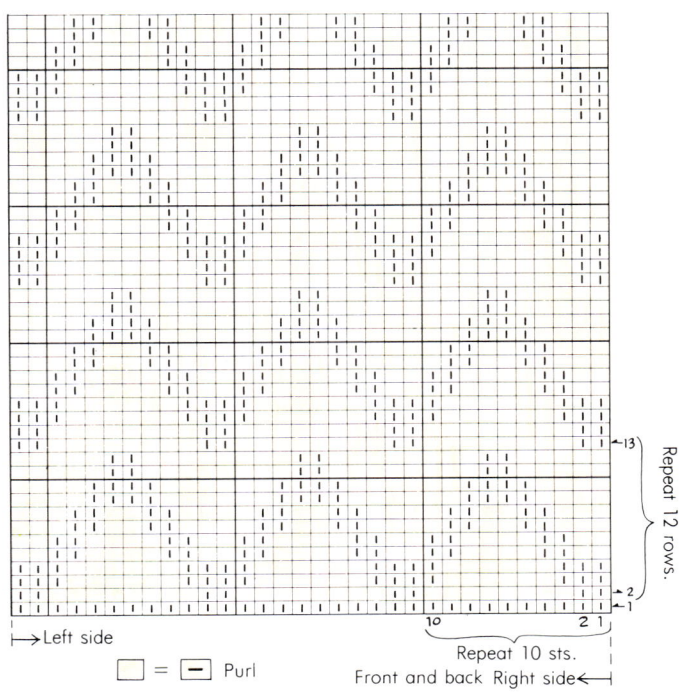

(1) Cast on 102 sts and work to armholes.

Pick up 102 sts through loops of chain (see page 30) and work even in pattern st with No. 7 needles to 79th row.

Chart for pattern

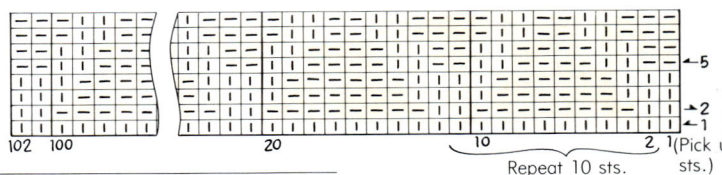

(2) Shape armholes.

Work first row of armholes with wrong side facing to last 6 sts. Place these 6 sts onto a holder. Work 2nd row to last 6 sts and place them onto holder as for first row. Work even from 3rd row to 51st row.

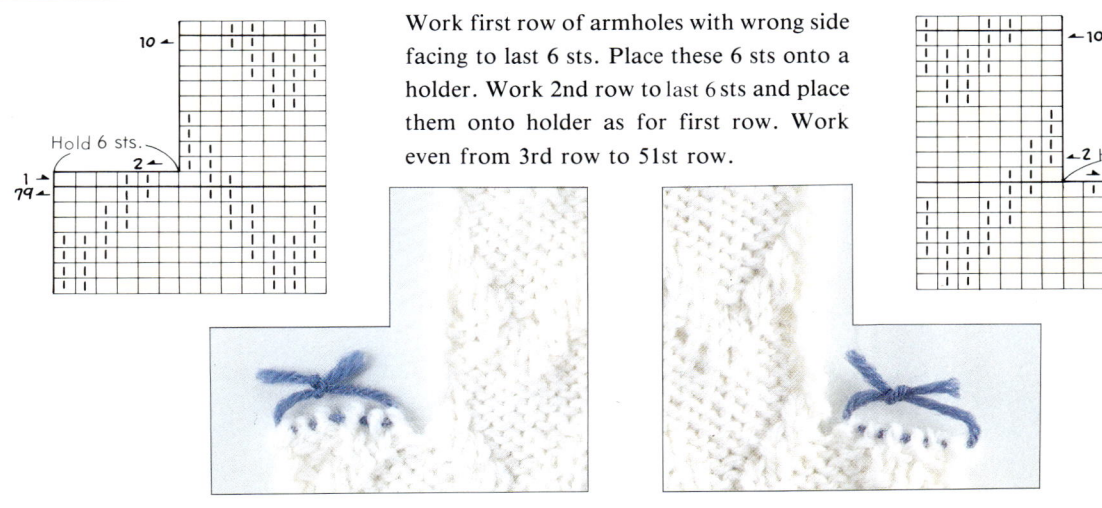

(3) Shape neck.

Work for left shoulder first. Work 35 sts and hold these sts for right shoulder. Bind off next 20 sts. Then start working for left shoulder. Shape neck decreasing as shown until 6th row of neck and hold 30 sts. Attach yarn at neck edge and work for right shoulder until 5th row and hold 30 sts.

See pages 6 and 7 for decreasing.
See page 10 for binding off.

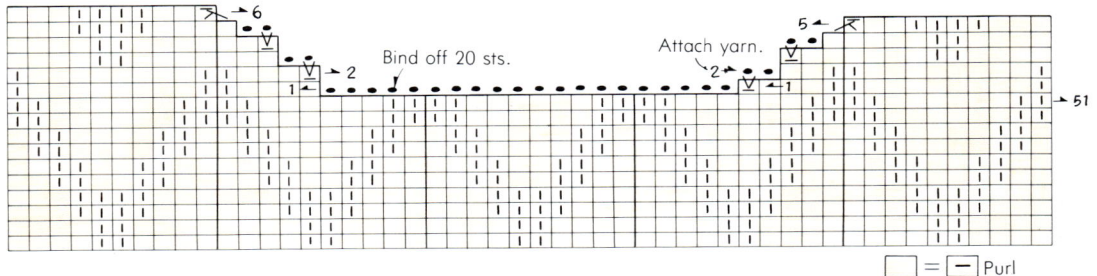

(4) Bottomband.

Change to No. 5 needles and pick up 94 sts decreasing 8 sts evenly spaced (see page 31 for decreasing). Work in K2, P2 rib to 20th row and bind off in rib.

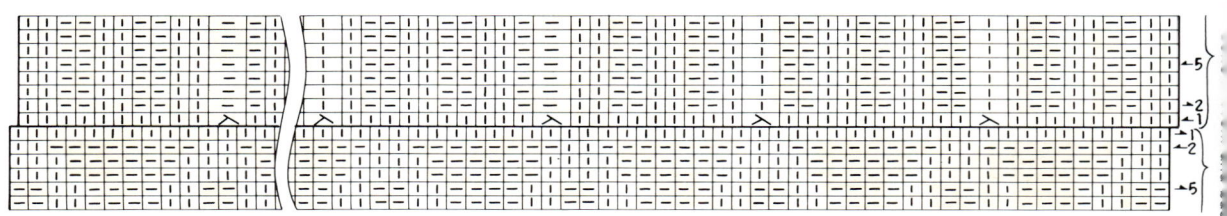

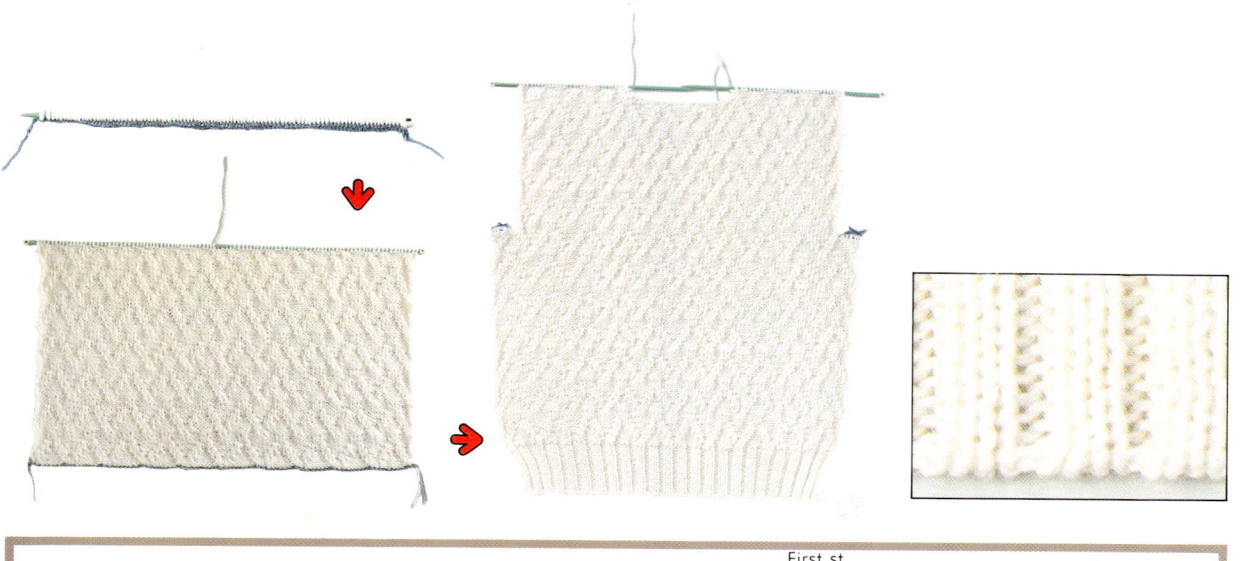

How to fasten off in K2, P2 rib
(using straight needles)

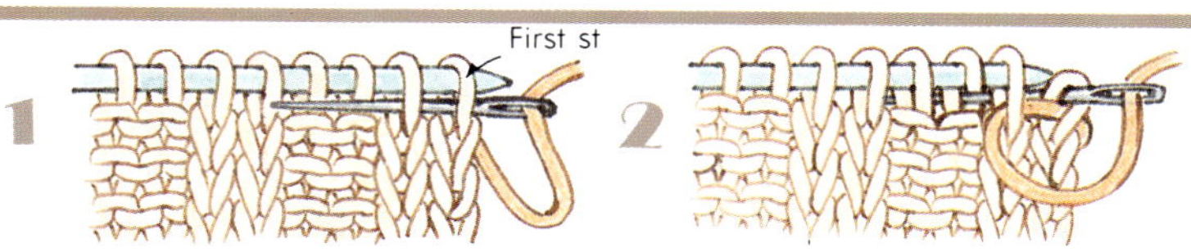

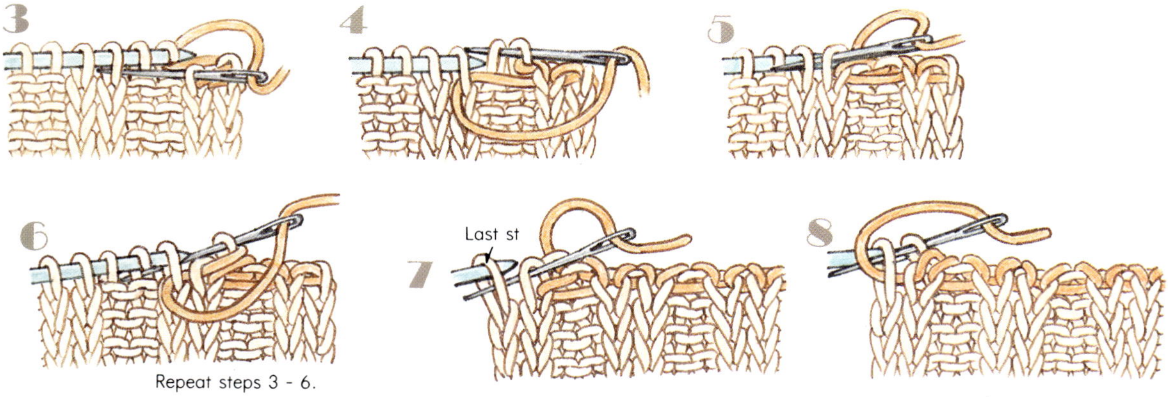

Repeat steps 3 - 6.

(using circular needle)

Repeat steps 2 - 5.

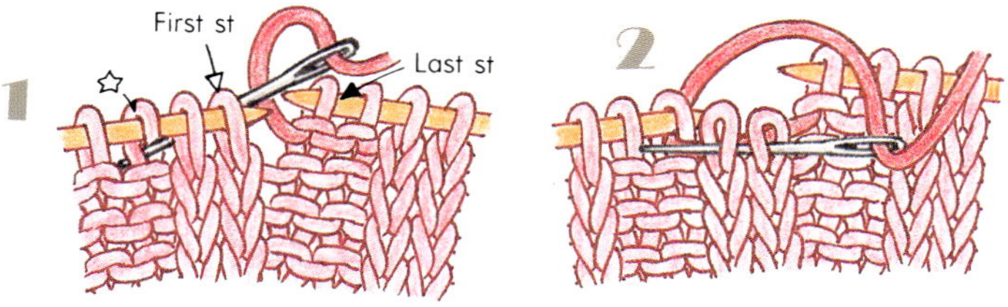

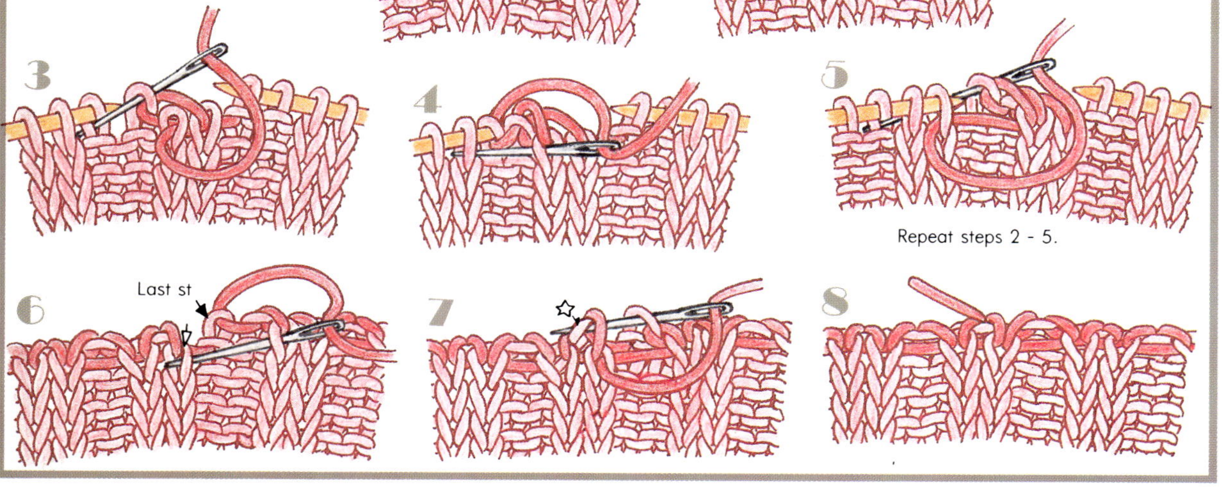

Front

(1) Work as for back.

Cast on 102 sts as for back and work in pattern st to 79th row.

(2) Shape armholes and neck.

Hold 6 sts each for right and left sides as for back. After working to 3rd row, shape right side first. Work 42 sts with right side facing and cast on 1 st for seam. Place center 6 sts onto a holder and hold remaining 42 sts for left side. Work even to 31st row, then shape neck following chart until 22nd row. Hold 30 sts. Attach yarn and cast on one st. Work for left side as for right side. Shape neck reversing right side but one row behind.

(3) Bottomband.

Pick up 94 sts as for back and work in K2, P2 rib (see page 40).

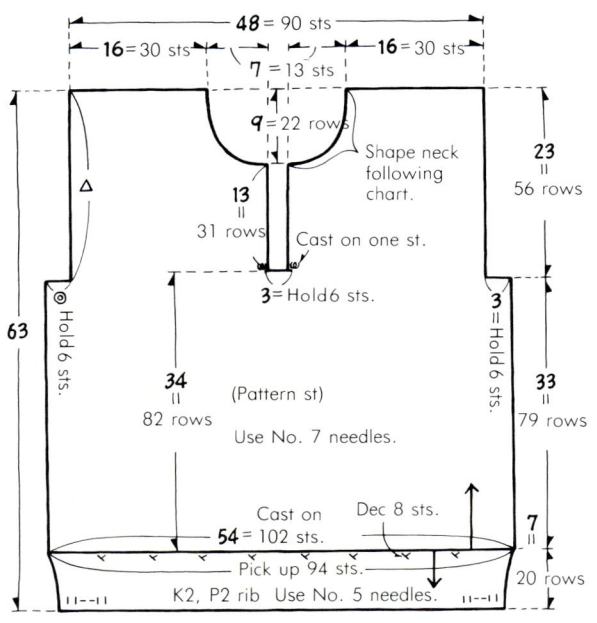

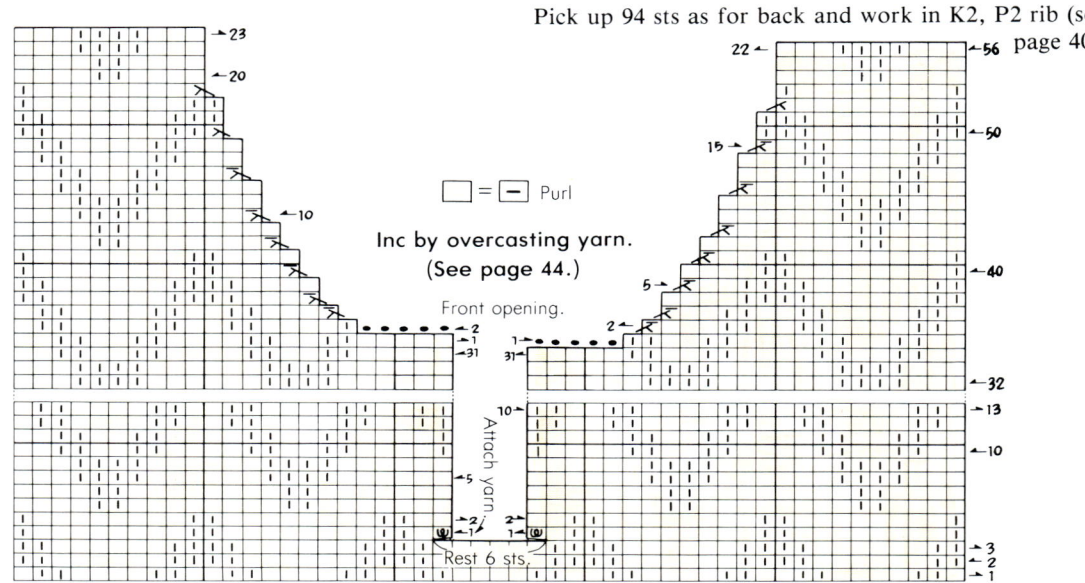

☐ = ⊟ Purl

Inc by overcasting yarn. (See page 44.)

Finishing

(1) Neckband.

Steam-press front and back. Join shoulder seams with crocheted slip stitch. Pick up 84 sts around neck with No. 5 needle starting at right front neck. Pick up 26 sts each from right and left fronts and 32 sts from back. Work in K2, P2 rib for 8 rows, but always work first 3 sts in st st. Bind off in rib.

(2) Front tab.

Pick up 35 sts along left front edge for tab and cast on one st at the end. Work in K2, P2 rib to 8th row making 2 buttonholes on 5th row. Bind off in rib. Cast on one st at the beginning of row and pick up 35 sts along right front edge for tab and work in rib as for left side without making buttonholes. Join end of left front tab and 6 hold sts. Sew end of right tab to wrong side of left tab. Sew on buttons.

See page 35 for crocheted slip stitch.
See page 41 for binding off in K2, P2 rib.

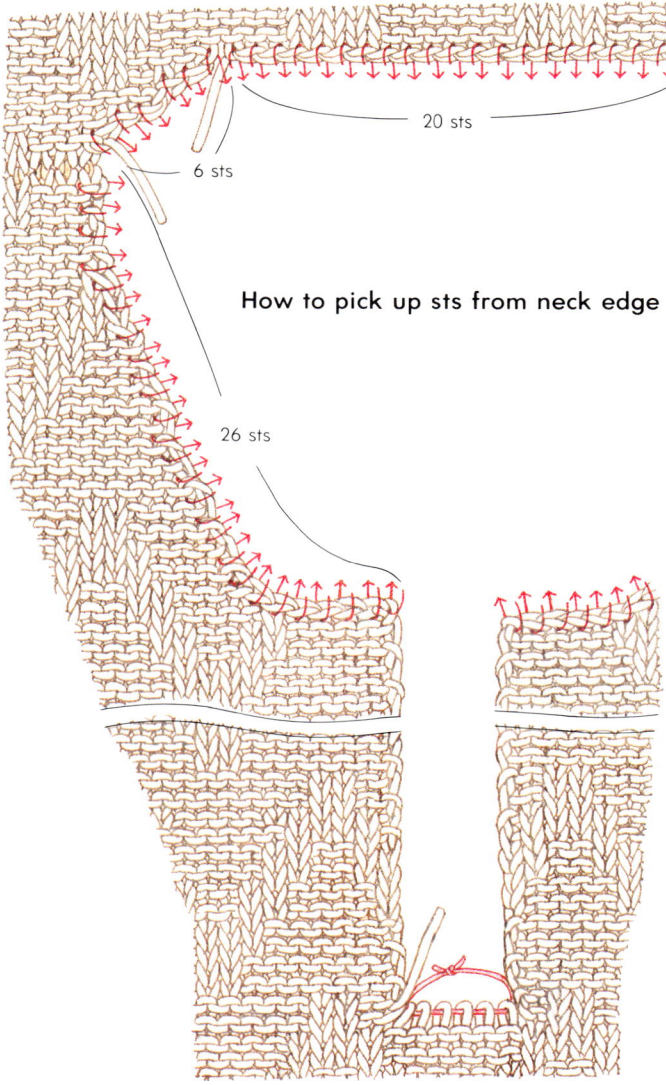

How to pick up sts from neck edge

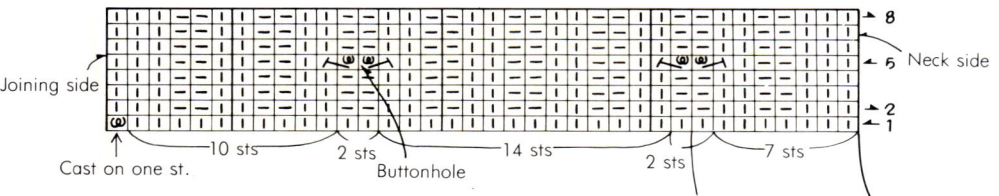

Front tab

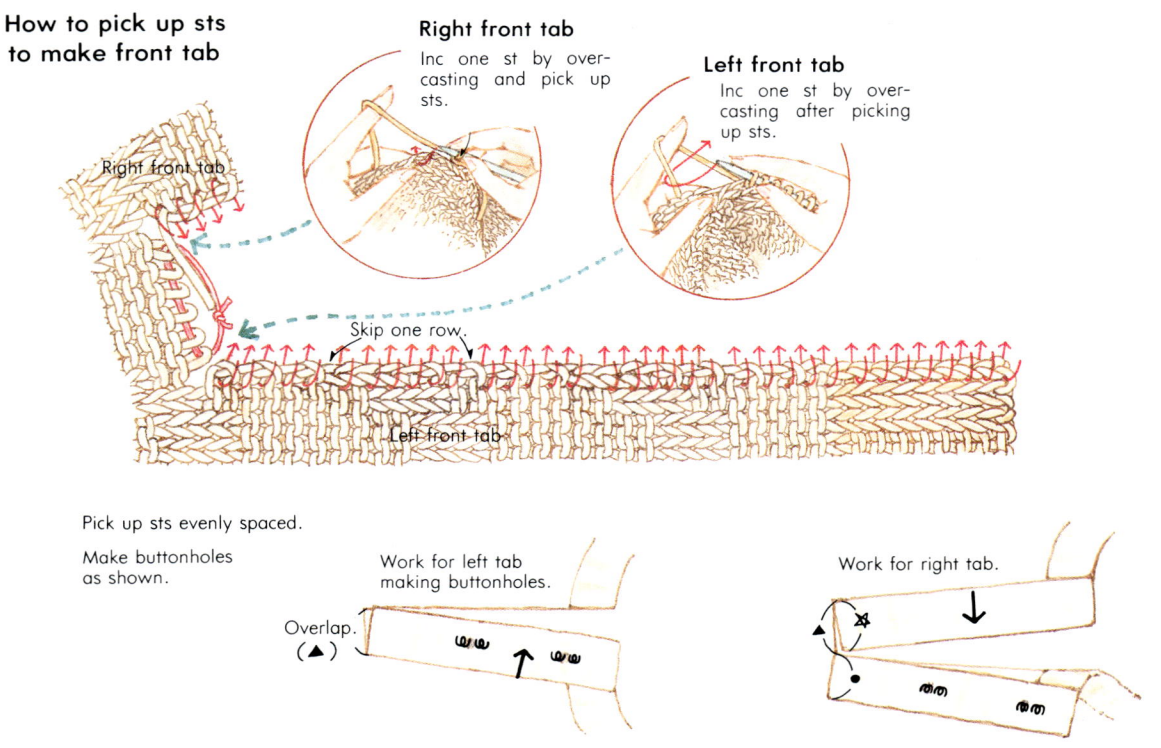

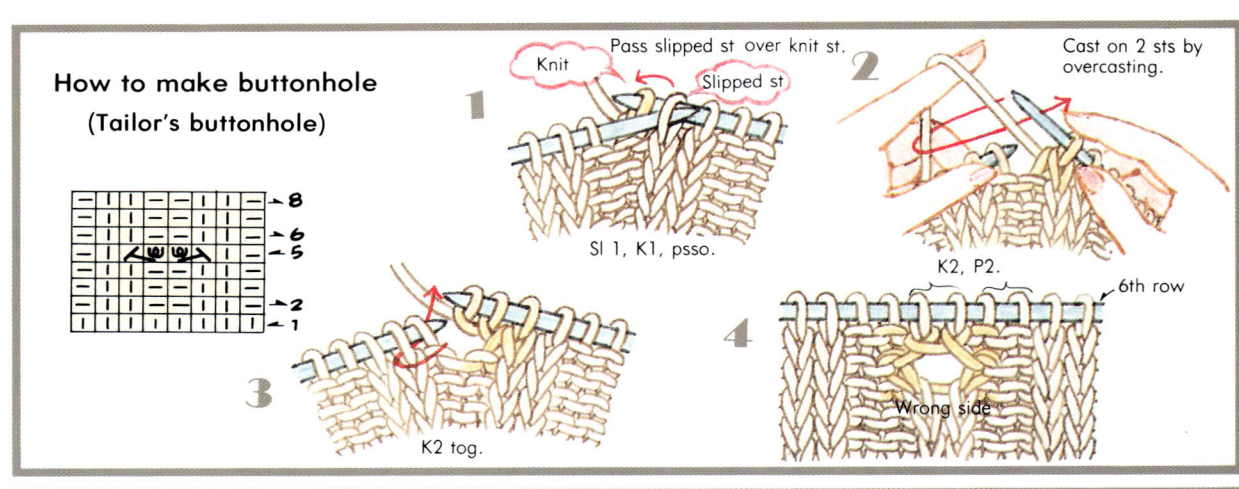

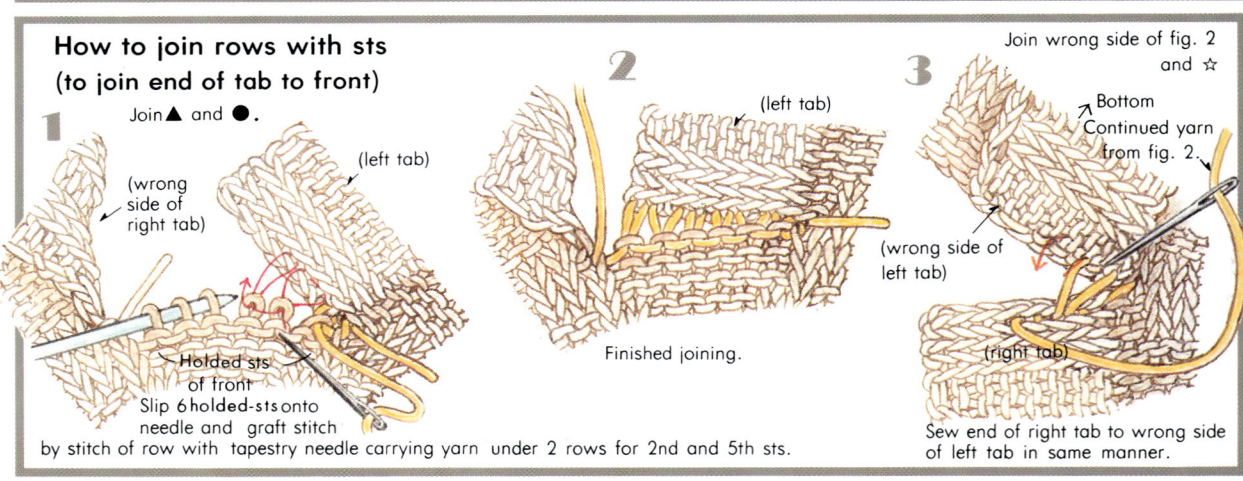

Sleeves

(1) Pick up sts along armholes and work for sleeves.

Pick up 88 sts from △ and ▲. Cast on 1 st at each side to make 90 sts. Work in pattern until 120th row decreasing at each side as shown on chart. Dec 14 sts evenly across row on 121st row — 42 sts left, and work in K2, P2 rib to 20th row. Bind off in rib. Work in same manner for second sleeve. See page 41 for binding off in K2, P2 rib.

How to pick up sts along armhole for sleeve

Pick up 3 sts from 3 rows and skip one row.
Pick up 4 sts from 4 rows and skip one row.
Pick up 4 sts from 4 rows and cast on one st.

Repeat these rows alternately.

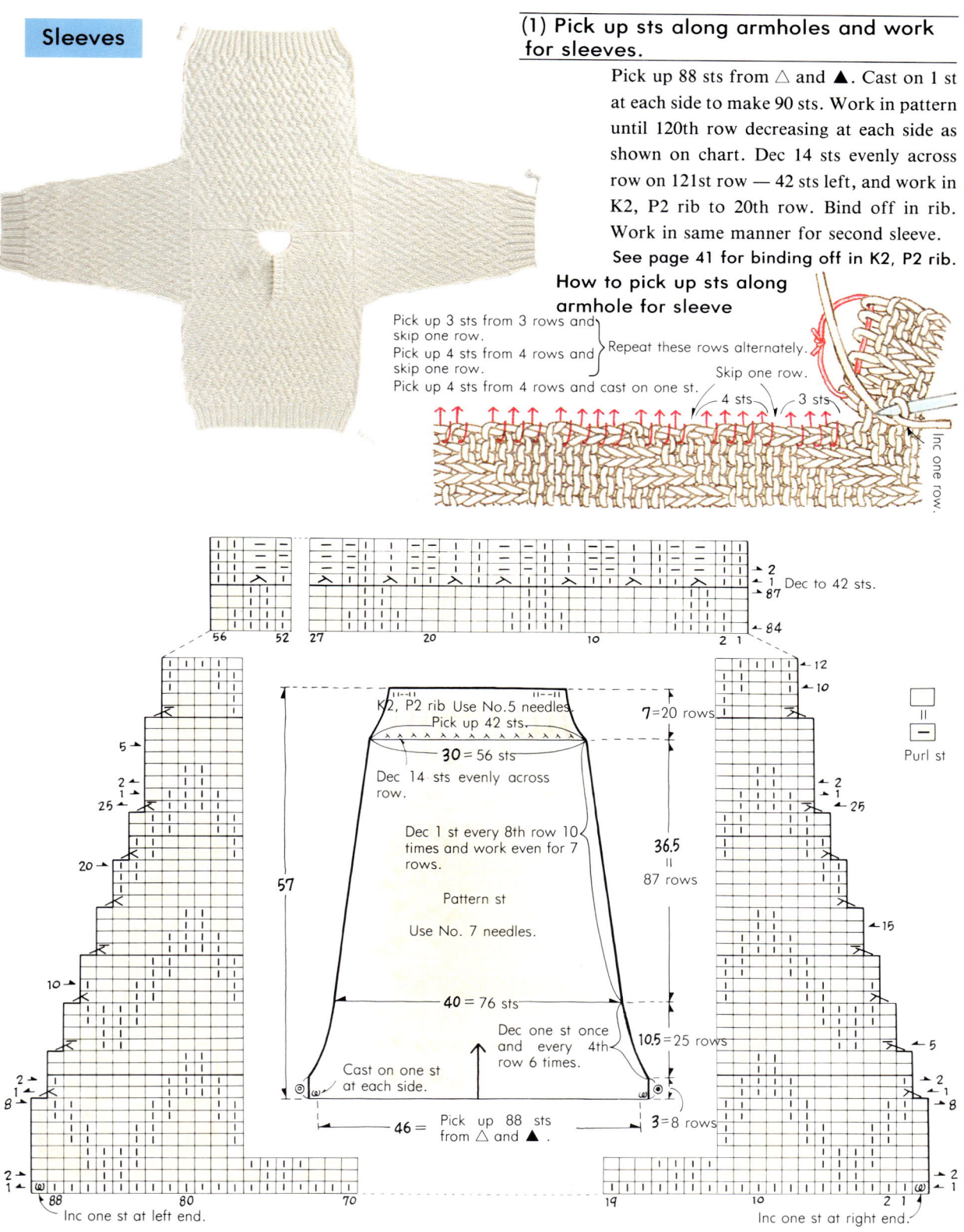

(2) Join side and underarm seams.

Block sleeves with **steam** iron. Match ◎ and ⊙ marks with those of front and back and join in same manner as shown on page 44. Join side and underarm seams with invisible seams (see page 36). Weave ends of yarn into knitting (see page 5). Steam-press the finished sweater.

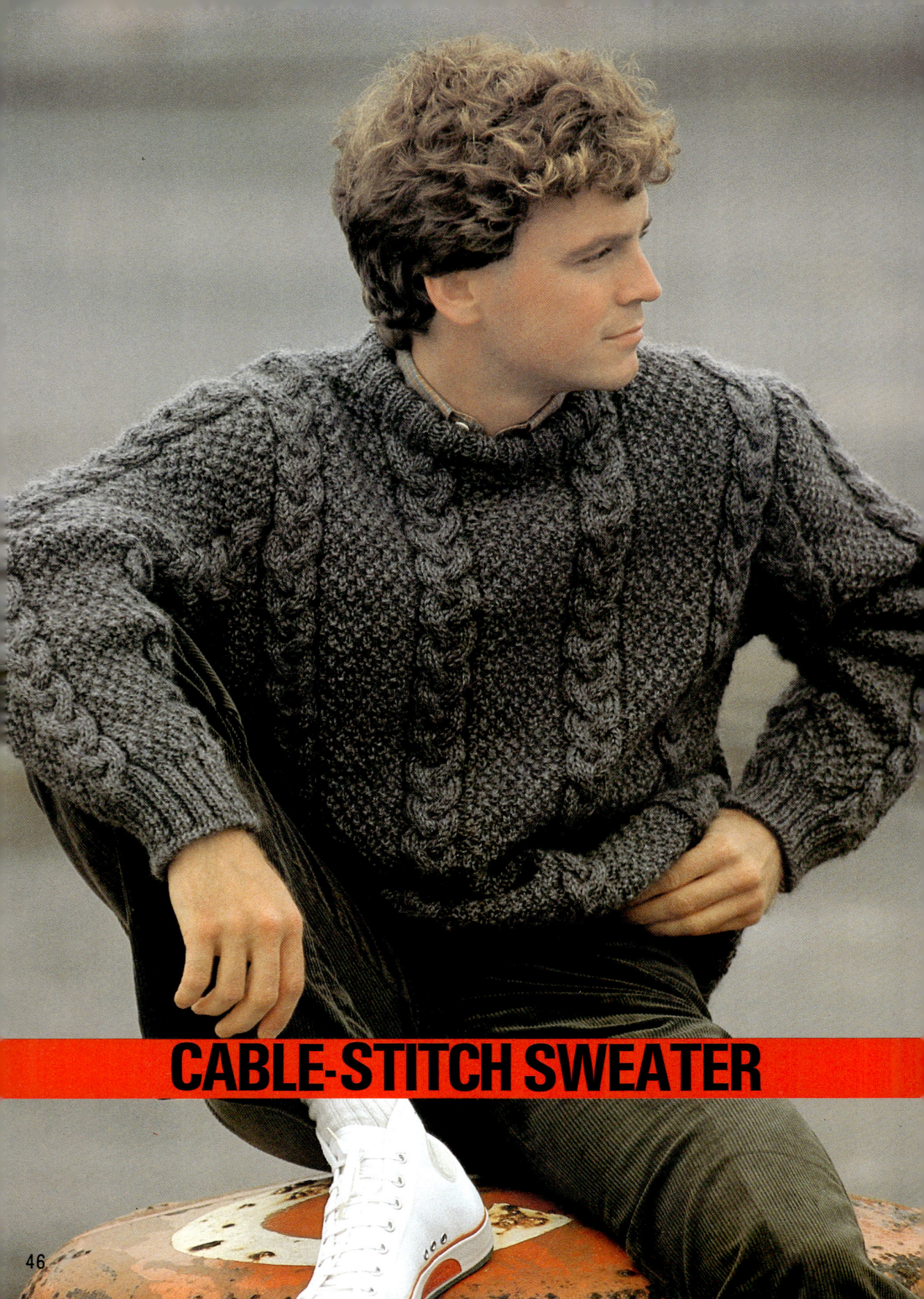

CABLE-STITCH SWEATER

Prepare the followings.

MATERIALS: Bulky yarn (100% wool, 2oz.=86yds): gray, 970g.
EQUIPMENT: Knitting needles: No. 5 (3.9mm) one set each of two and four; No. 7 (4.5mm) one set of two. Cable needle. Crochet hook size 5/F or 6/G (4.0mm). Stitch holders. Markers.

Finished size

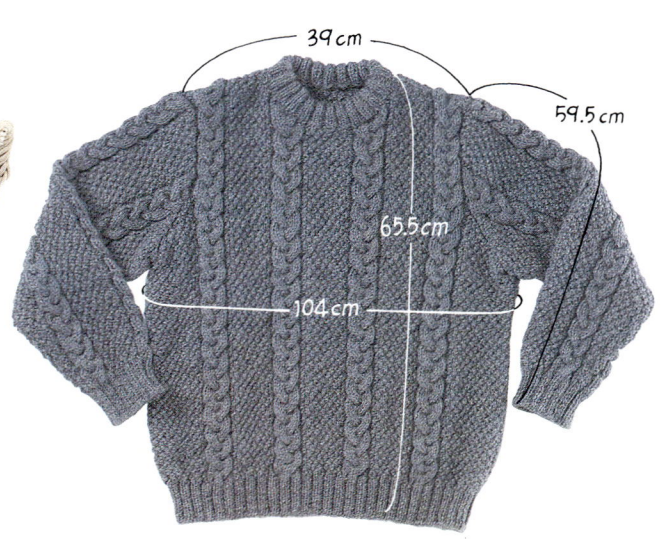

GAUGE

22 sts = 10cm; 24 rows = 10cm in pattern st.

Cable and seed patterns are traditionally popular and yet still have a contemporary look. It will take less time to make this sweater than you think.

Back

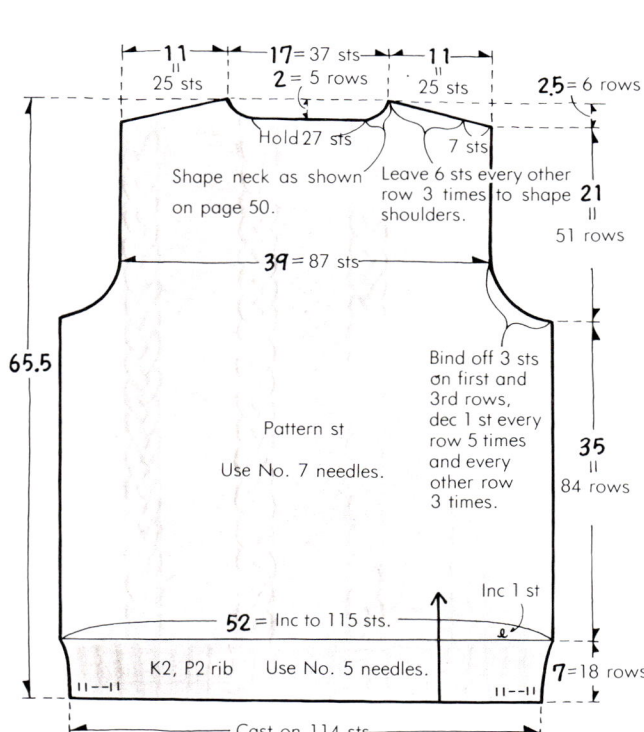

(1) Cast on 114 sts and work in K2, P2 rib.

Ch 114 and pick up sts through loops of chain as shown below. Work even in K2, P2 rib to 18th row.

Chart for K2, P2 rib.

Right side
Left side
5
2
1
Casting on
114
110
10
5
2 1

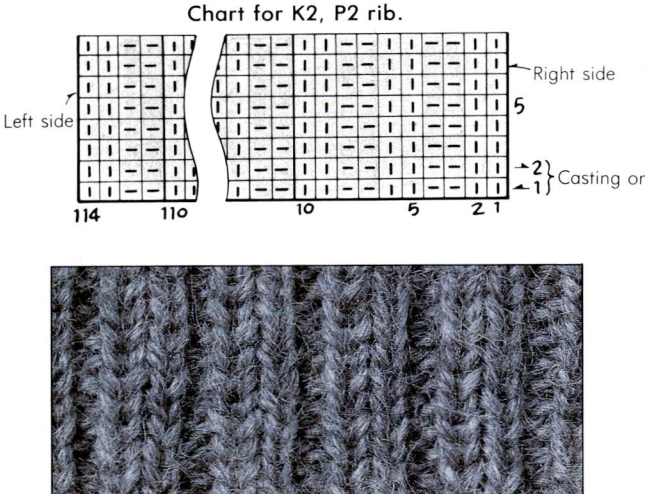

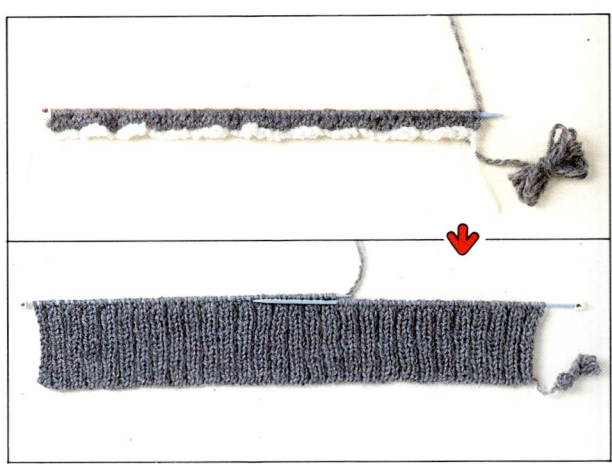

How to cast on sts for K2, P2 rib

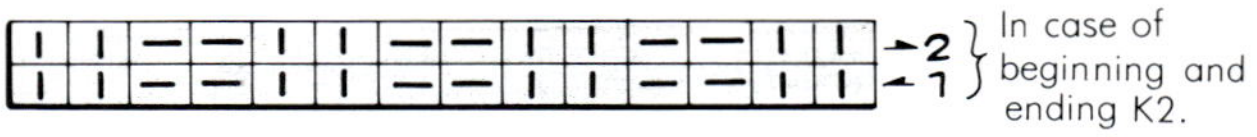

2
1
In case of beginning and ending K2.

1

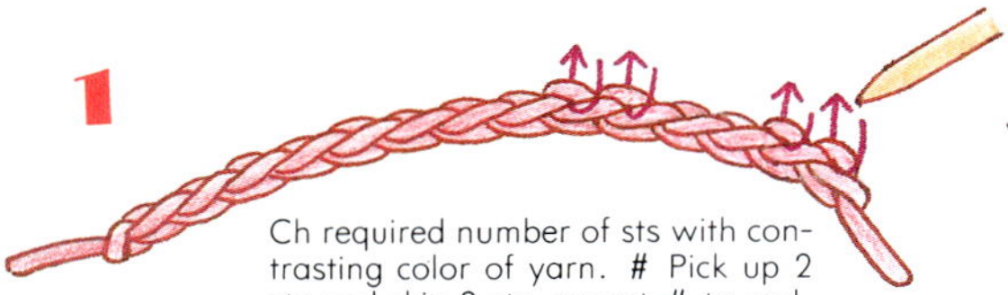

Ch required number of sts with contrasting color of yarn. # Pick up 2 sts and skip 2 sts, repeat # to end.

2

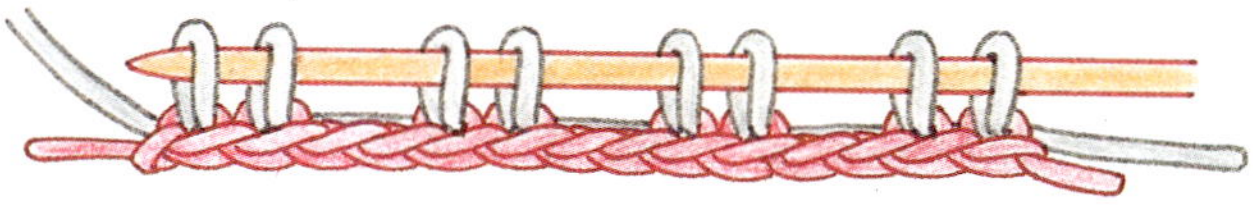

3

Knit
Purl

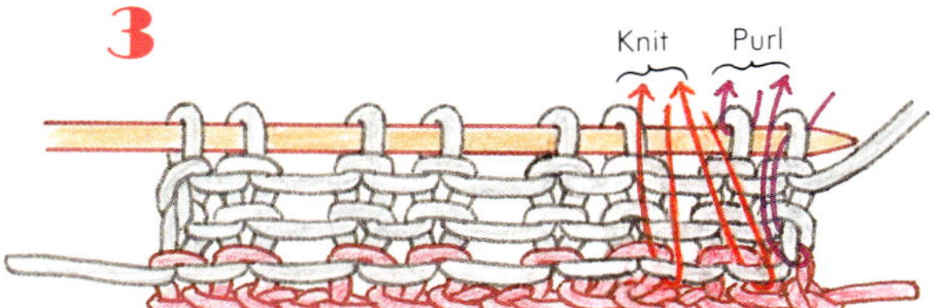

Work for 2 rows in st st, turn, then K2, P2 alternately, inserting needle into sts as the arrows show.

4

Knit
Purl
Knit
Purl

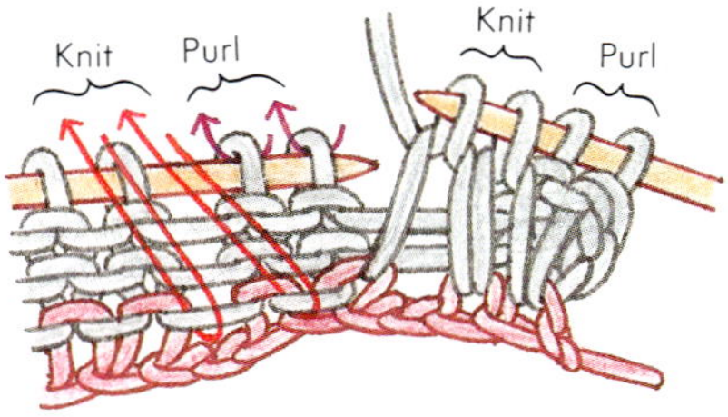

5

Purl

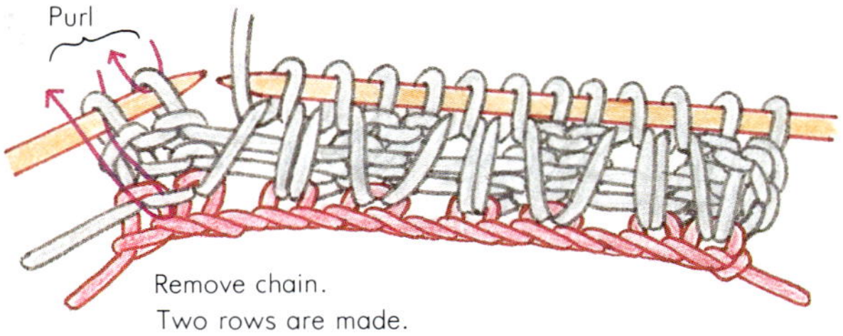

Remove chain.
Two rows are made.

(2) Work even to 84th row.

Change to No. 7 needles. Inc 1 st (= 115 sts) and work even in pattern st to 84th row.

See page 12 for increasing.

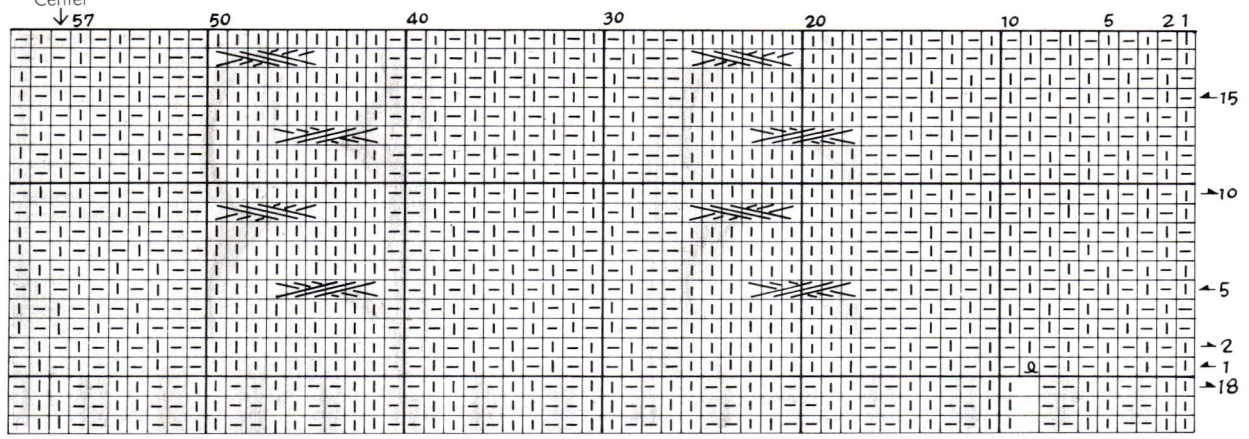

Chart for pattern

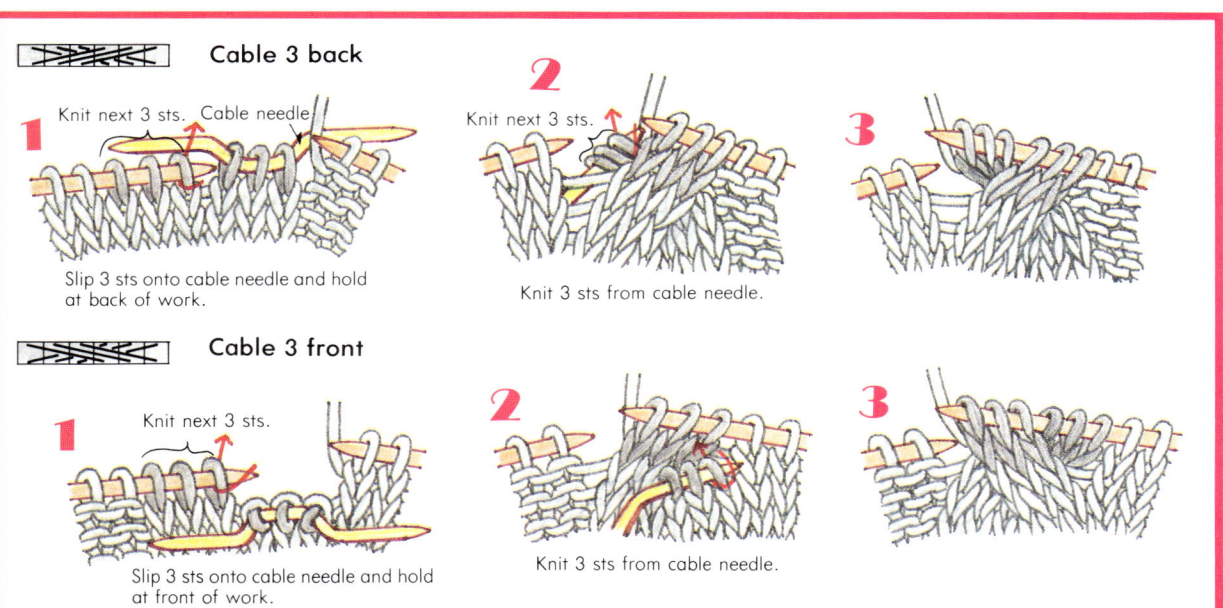

Cable 3 back

1. Slip 3 sts onto cable needle and hold at back of work.
2. Knit next 3 sts.
3. Knit 3 sts from cable needle.

Cable 3 front

1. Slip 3 sts onto cable needle and hold at front of work.
2. Knit next 3 sts.
3. Knit 3 sts from cable needle.

(3) Shape armholes, neck and shoulders.

After working to 84th row in pattern st, shape armholes following chart. Work even for 37 rows after decreasing for 14 rows. Shape right shoulder in same manner as shown on pages 8 and 9. Place 30 sts on left side onto needle and 27 sts at center back onto a holder. Leave all the stitches of right shoulder on needle after shaping and cut yarn leaving about 40cm. Attach yarn at neck edge and shape left shoulder in same manner.

See pages 6 and 7 for decreasing.
See pages 8 and 9 for shaping shoulders.

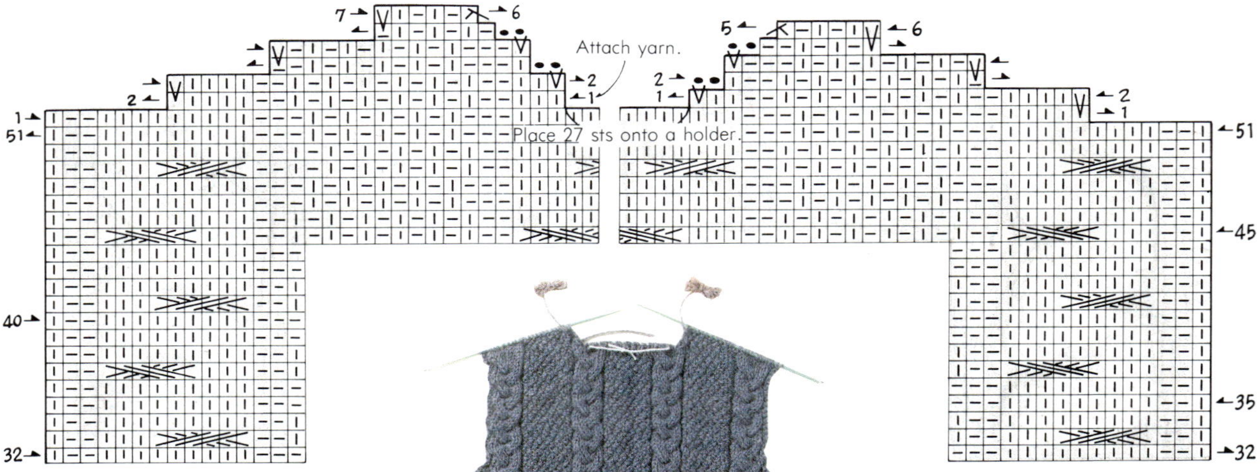

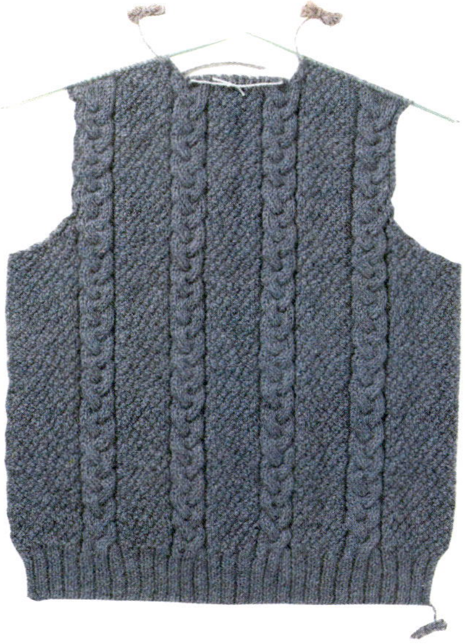

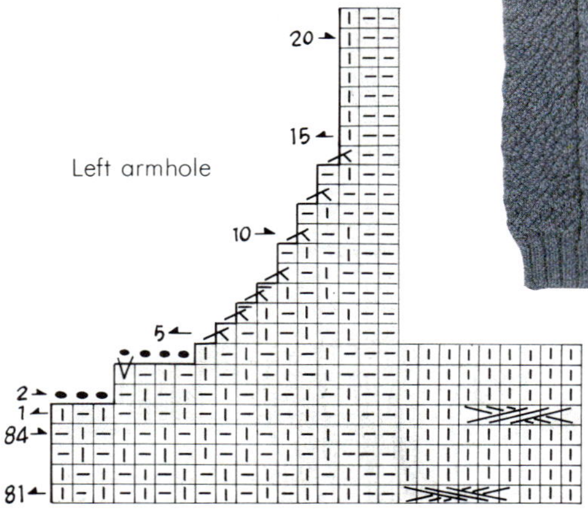

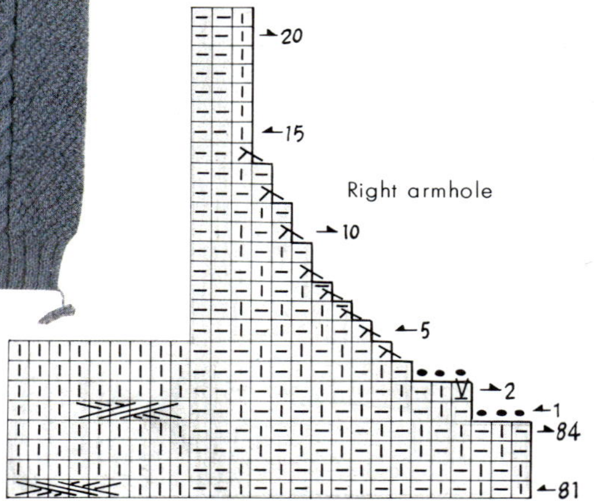

Attach yarn.
Place 27 sts onto a holder.
7
6
2
1
51
45
40
35
32
5

Left armhole
20
15
10
5
2
1
84
81

Right armhole
20
15
10
5
2
1
84
81

How to wash hand knits
Before washing, trace outline of sweater on paper.
Use luke warm water and detergent for woolens.
Squeeze sweater very gently.
Fold sweater as shown and spin-dry for 20-30 seconds.
Rinse thoroughly (at least twice), squeezing very gently.
Spin-dry again.
Place sweater on traced paper.
Dry flat on a towel or board placed in the shade or inside.
Steam-press.

2
1
51
40
33

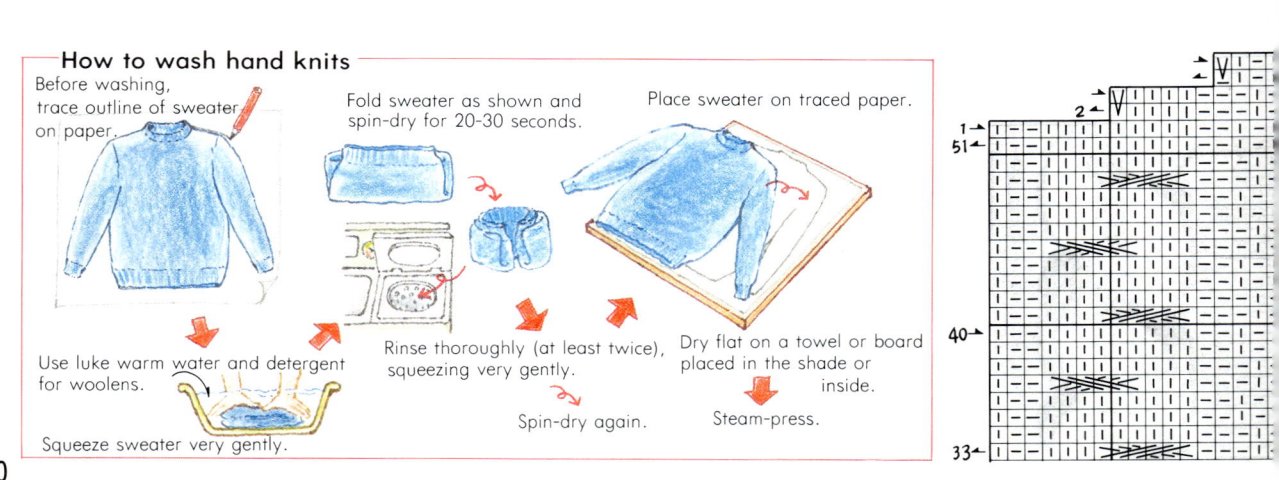

Front

1) Cast on 114 sts and work in rib and pattern.

Cast on 114 sts in same manner as for back and work in K2, P2 rib to 18th row. Inc one st and work in pattern st to 84th row. Notice that first row of front and last row of back made seed st pattern.

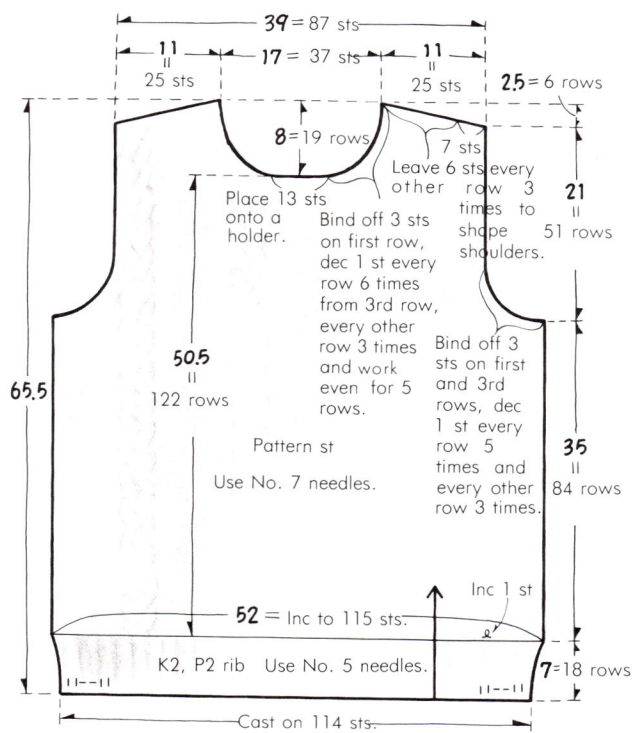

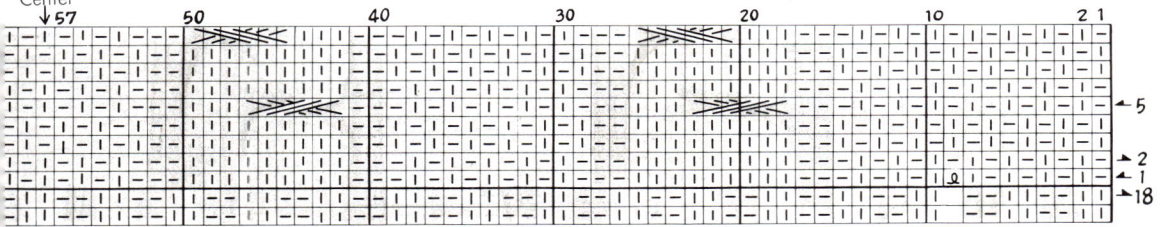

Chart for pattern

2) Shape armholes, neck and shoulders.

Shape armholes as for back and work even to 38th row. Shape neck following chart. Shape shoulders as shown on pages 8 and 9. Attach yarn at neck edge and work for left side as for right side.

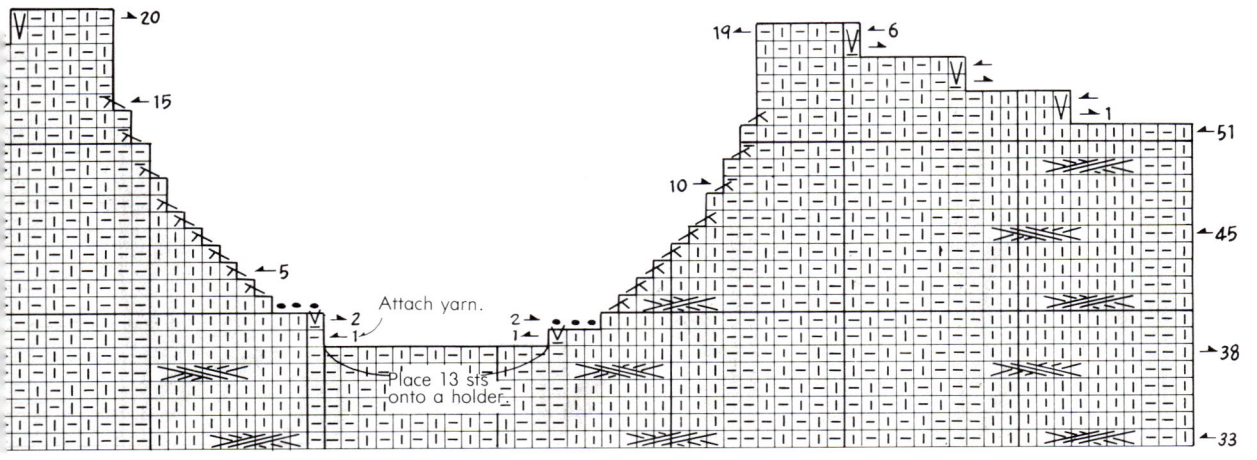

Sleeves

(1) Cast on 58 sts and work in rib.

Cast on 58 sts as for front and work in K2, P2 rib for 18 rows.

(2) Work in pattern st.

Inc 9 sts on first row (= 67 sts). Work in pattern st to 96th row increasing 1 st at each side. Dec following chart to shape sleeve cap. Bind off 23 sts on last row.

See page 10 for binding off.

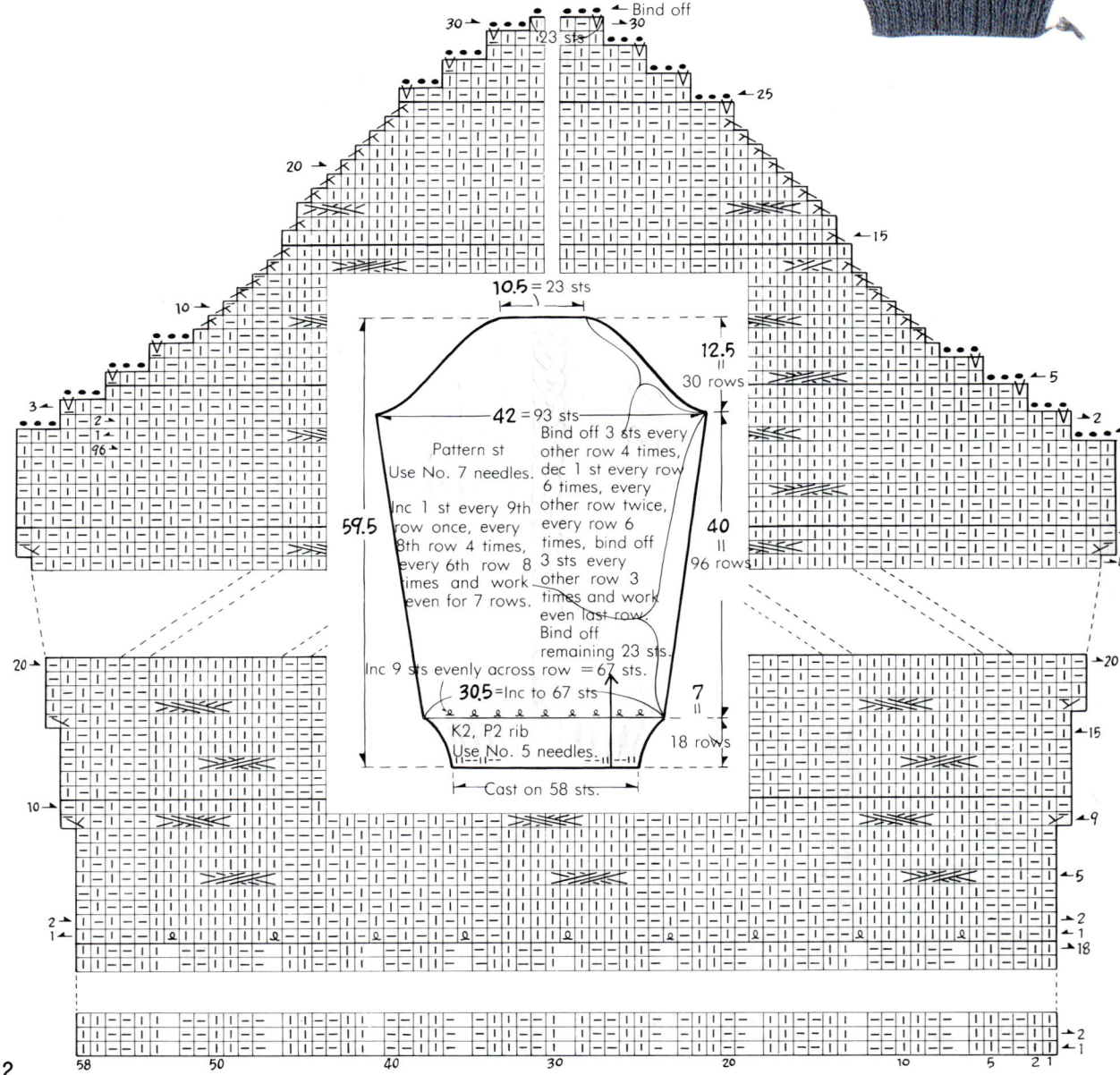

Finishing

Join shoulders with crocheted slip stitch.

How to sew neck edge to wrong side

Method A: Grafting

Being elastic, this is a suitable method when joining neck edge.

1
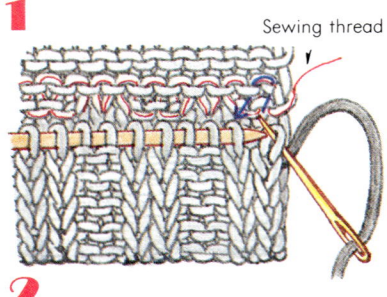
Sewing thread

2
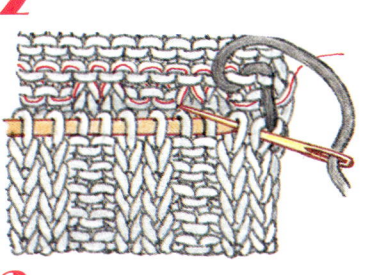

3
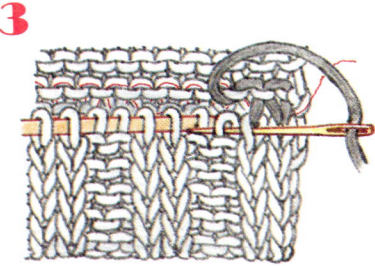

4

(1) Steam-press.

Before joining seams, steam-press carefully so as not to stretch knit pieces.

See page 14 for steam-pressing.

(2) Join shoulder seams.

With right sides of front and back facing, work crocheted slip stitch loosely.

See page 35 for crocheted slip stitch.

(3) Neckband.

With No. 5 needles, work in K2, P2 rib for 16 rounds, fold in half and sew to wrong side as shown.

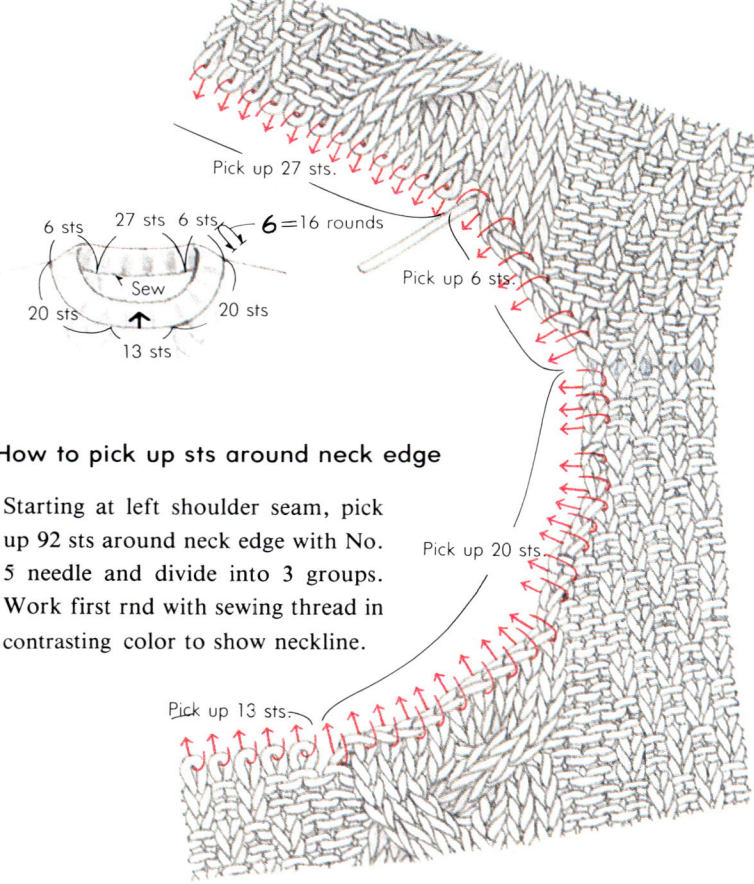

How to pick up sts around neck edge

Starting at left shoulder seam, pick up 92 sts around neck edge with No. 5 needle and divide into 3 groups. Work first rnd with sewing thread in contrasting color to show neckline.

Method B: Slip-stitching

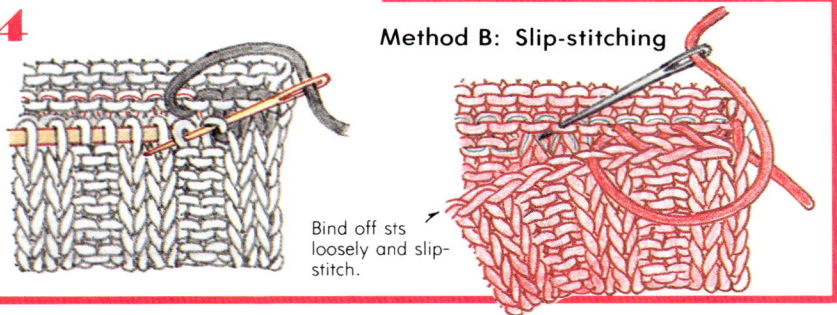

Bind off sts loosely and slip-stitch.

(4) Join side and underarm seams.

Using remaining yarn used for casting on, join side and underarm seams with invisible seams. Draw yarn gently after every stitch is worked.

Invisible seams

How to join side seam of K2, P2 rib

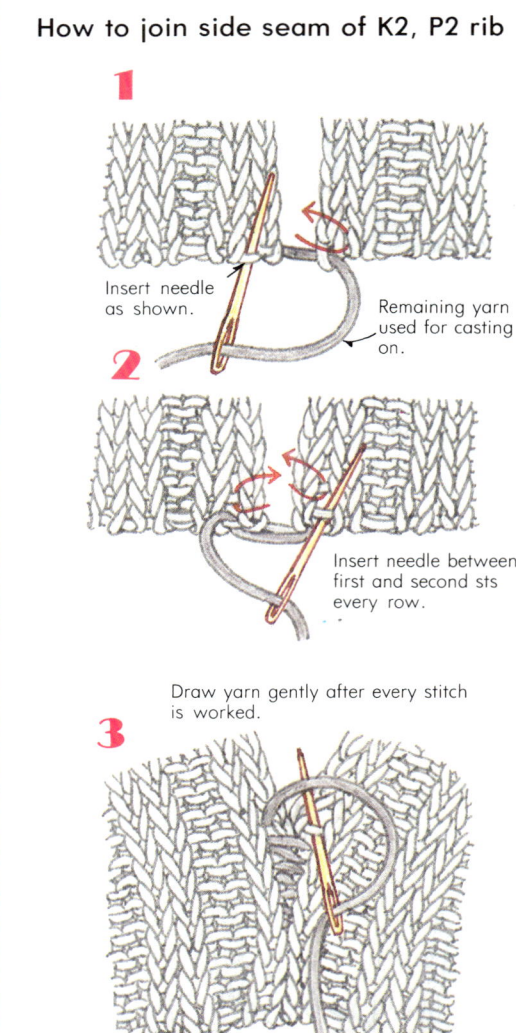

1 Insert needle as shown. Remaining yarn used for casting on.

2 Insert needle between first and second sts every row.

3 Draw yarn gently after every stitch is worked.

(5) Set sleeves in.

Turn body to wrong side. Insert sleeve into armhole with right sides facing and pin. Work crocheted slip stitch with one strand of yarn, starting at side seam. Steam-press.

You can do it and it is fun!!

Illustrated Basic Crochet & Knit

A colorful, handy book, fully illustrated, with step-by-step directions for all basic crochet and knitting stitches and techniques. A treasure-trove for beginners.

48pp; 7¼ × 10¼ in.
ISBN 0-87040-389-3

Prepare the followings.

MATERIALS: Bulky yarn (100% wool, 2oz. = 86yds): navy blue, 680g.
EQUIPMENT: Knitting needles: No. 5 (3.9mm) one set each of two and four; No. 7 (4.5mm) one set of two. Crochet hook size 5/F or 6/G (4.0mm). Tapestry needle. Stitch holders. Markers.

Finished size

GAUGE
16 sts = 10 cm; 20 rows = 10 cm in st st.

This is also knitted in basic stitches. Emblem or initials will add a delightful accent to the simple cardigan.

Back

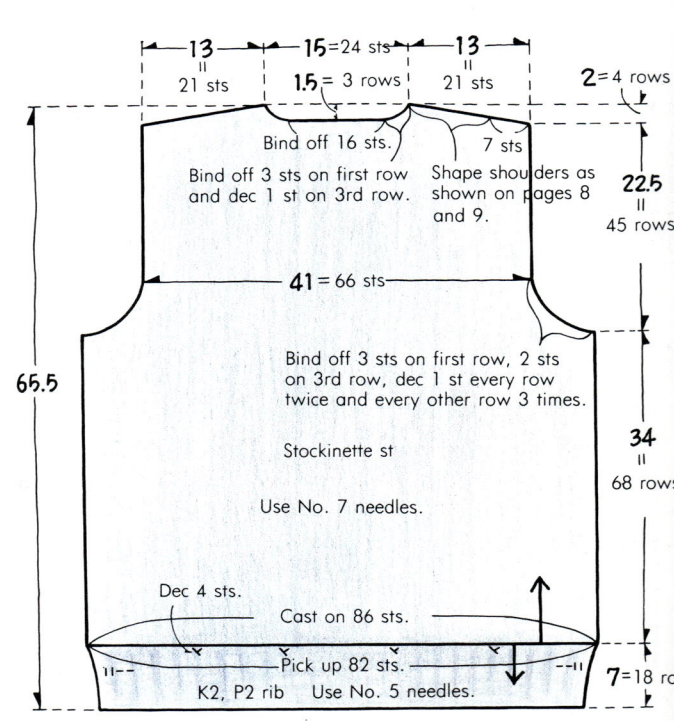

(1) Cast on 86 sts using chain which is later removed.

Work even in st st for 68 rows using No. 7 needles.

See page 30 for casting on through loops of chain.

(2) Shape armholes, shoulders and neck.

Shape armholes following chart and work even for 34 rows. Work first row of shoulder with wrong side facing to last 7 sts, turn, Sl 1, K 17, bind off 16 sts at center back loosely and work for left shoulder, shaping as shown on pages 8 and 9. Leave 40cm of yarn and cut off. Attach yarn at neck edge and work the right shoulder in same manner.

See pages 6 and 7 for decreasing.
See pages 8 and 9 for shaping shoulders.

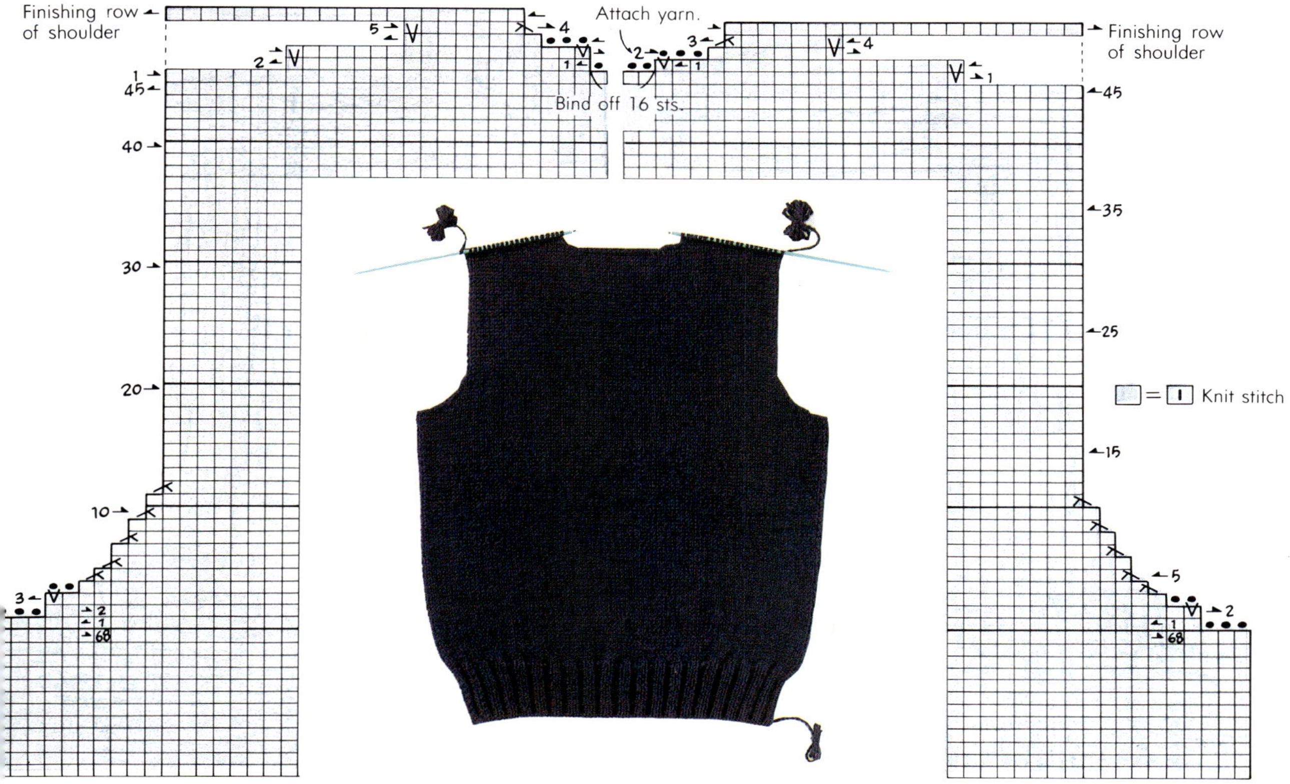

3) Bottomband.

Pick up 82 sts (dec 4 sts from cast-on sts) with No. 5 needle. Work in K2, P2 rib for 18 rows and bind off in rib.

See page 41 for fastening off in K2, P2 rib.
See page 31 for picking up from cast-on sts.

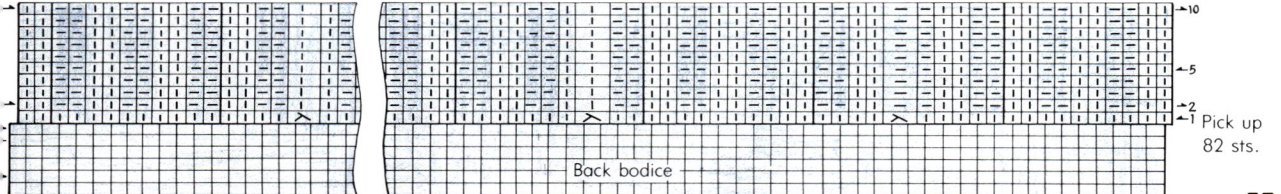

Front

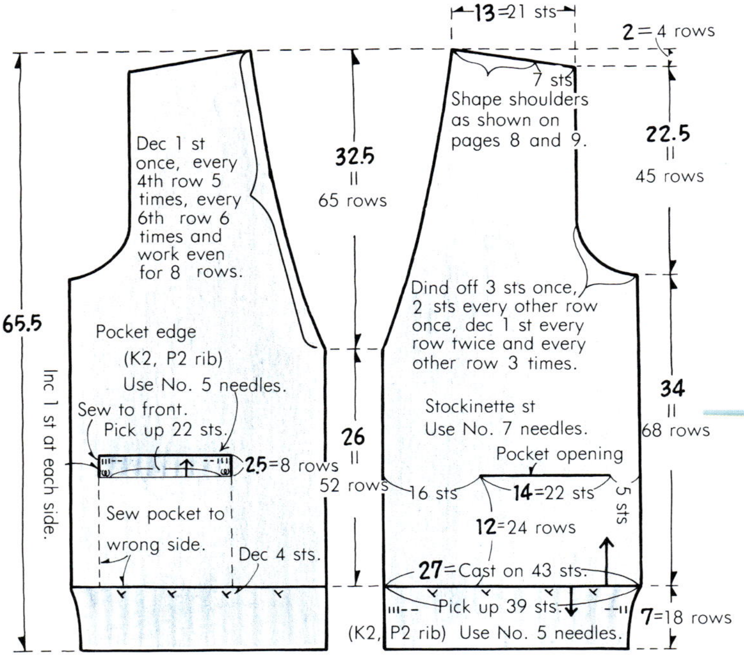

Left Front

(1) Cast on 43 sts.

Work for front as for back. Cast on 43 sts and work in st st for 24 rows with No. 7 needles. On 25th row, K 5, K 22 with contrasting yarn for pocket opening, then K 22 and K 16 with navy yarn. Work even for 28 rows.

(2) Shape neck, armholes and shoulders.

On 53rd row (first row of neck edge), start shaping neck. On 68th row (16th row of neck edge), start shaping armholes. On 45th row of armholes, start shaping shoulders in same manner as shown on pages 8 and 9.

(3) Bottomband.

Pick up 39 sts (dec 4 sts) from bottom edge, work in K2, P2 rib for 18 rows and bind off in rib.

Right front

Work as for left front reversing shaping.

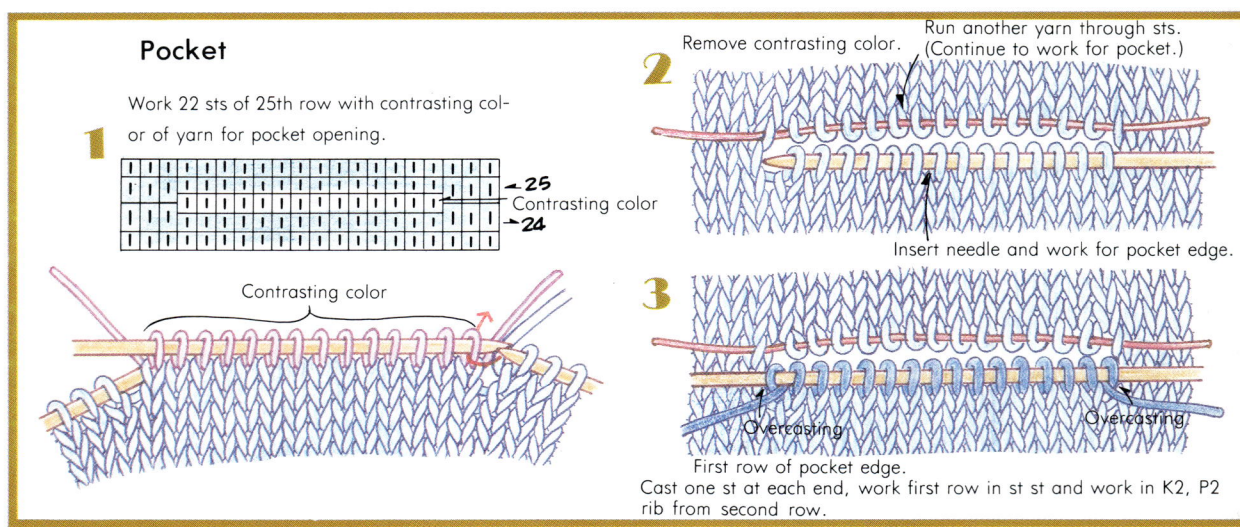

Pocket

1. Work 22 sts of 25th row with contrasting color of yarn for pocket opening.

2. Remove contrasting color. Run another yarn through sts. (Continue to work for pocket.) Insert needle and work for pocket edge.

3. Overcasting. First row of pocket edge. Cast one st at each end, work first row in st st and work in K2, P2 rib from second row.

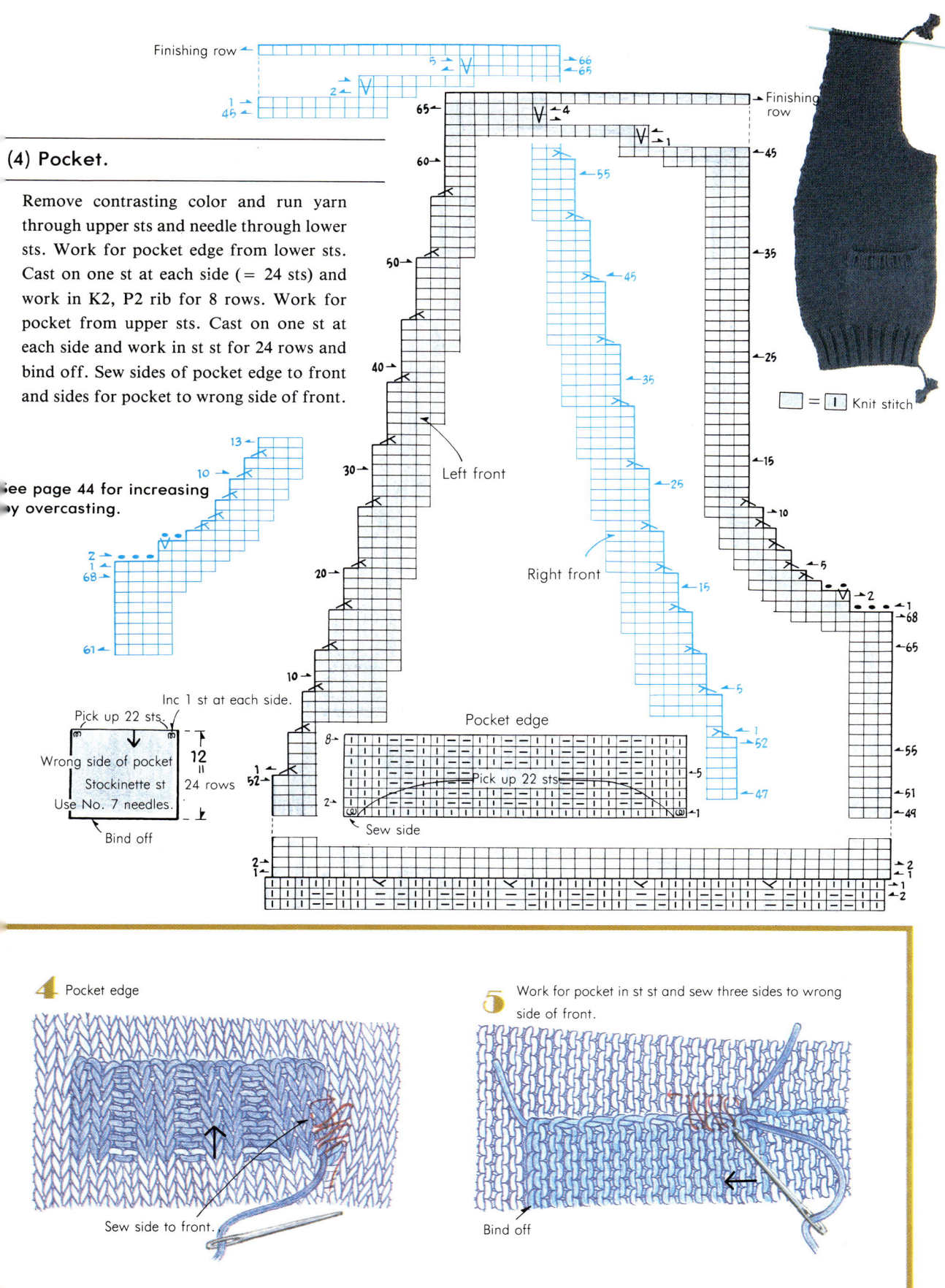

(4) Pocket.

Remove contrasting color and run yarn through upper sts and needle through lower sts. Work for pocket edge from lower sts. Cast on one st at each side (= 24 sts) and work in K2, P2 rib for 8 rows. Work for pocket from upper sts. Cast on one st at each side and work in st st for 24 rows and bind off. Sew sides of pocket edge to front and sides for pocket to wrong side of front.

See page 44 for increasing by overcasting.

4 Pocket edge
Sew side to front.

5 Work for pocket in st st and sew three sides to wrong side of front.
Bind off

Sleeves

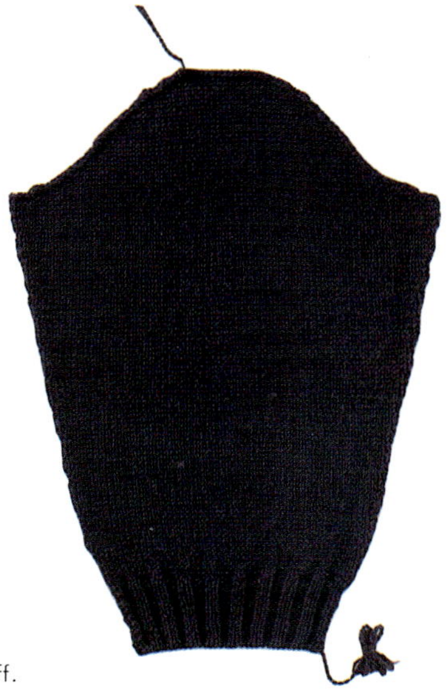

(1) Cast on 48 sts and work sleeves following chart below.

Cast on 48 sts as for back and work in st st for 80 rows increasing at each side. Dec to shape sleeve cap at beg of each row following chart. Bind off remaining sts after working 26th row.

   See pages 24 and 25 for increasing.
   See page 10 for binding off.

(2) Sleevebands.

Pick up 38 sts from bottom edge and work even in K2, P2 rib for 18 rows. Bind off in rib.

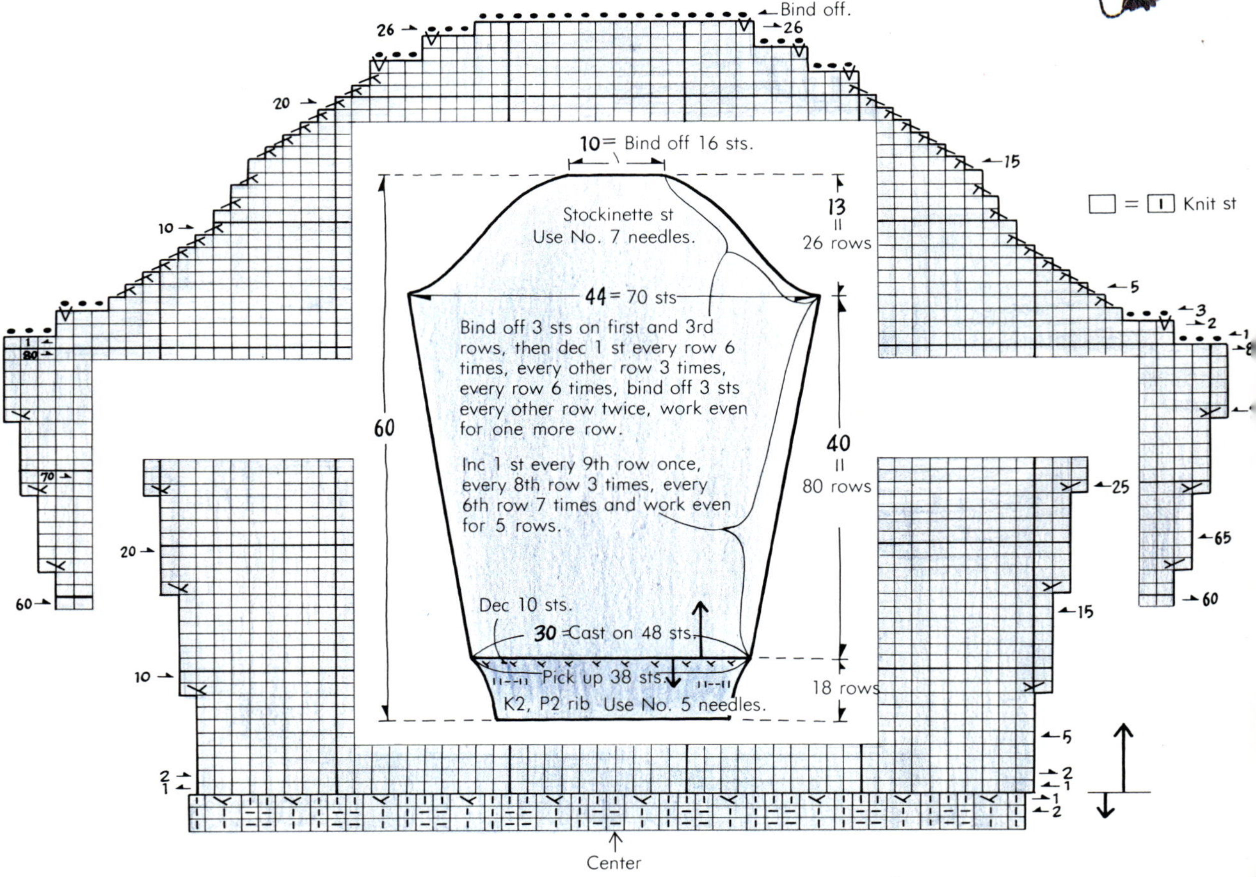

Stockinette st
Use No. 7 needles.

44 = 70 sts

Bind off 3 sts on first and 3rd rows, then dec 1 st every row 6 times, every other row 3 times, every row 6 times, bind off 3 sts every other row twice, work even for one more row.

Inc 1 st every 9th row once, every 8th row 3 times, every 6th row 7 times and work even for 5 rows.

Dec 10 sts.
30 = Cast on 48 sts.
Pick up 38 sts
K2, P2 rib Use No. 5 needles.

□ = ① Knit st

How to sew on button

Use double strands of heavy-duty silk thread in color matching button. Place smaller button on wrong side for reinforcement. After sewing buttons onto knitting, bring needle to front, loop thread around and tie knot. Cut off excess thread.

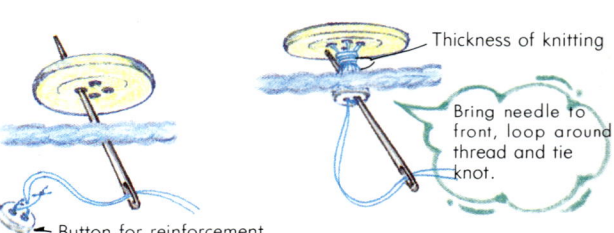

Thickness of knitting

Bring needle to front, loop around thread and tie knot.

← Button for reinforcement

Finishing

(1) Join shoulder seams.

With right sides facing, work crocheted slip stitch along shoulder seam (see page 35).

(2) Join side and underarm seams.

With right sides up, sew with invisible seams (see page 36).

(3) Neck and frontband.

With No. 5 needle, pick up 288 sts starting at bottom of right front around right and left fronts and neck. Divide into 3 groups and work in K2, P2 rib for 8 rows. Make buttonholes on left front.

How to pick up sts for front band

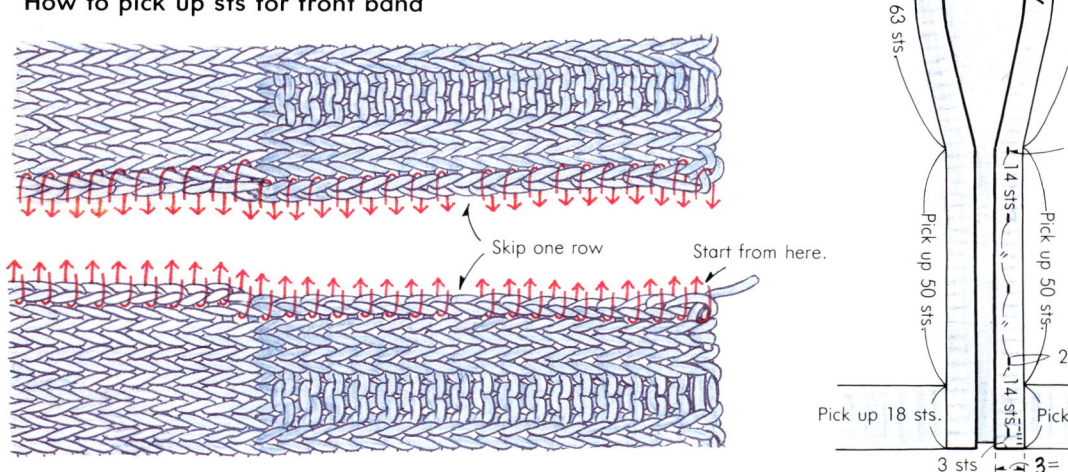

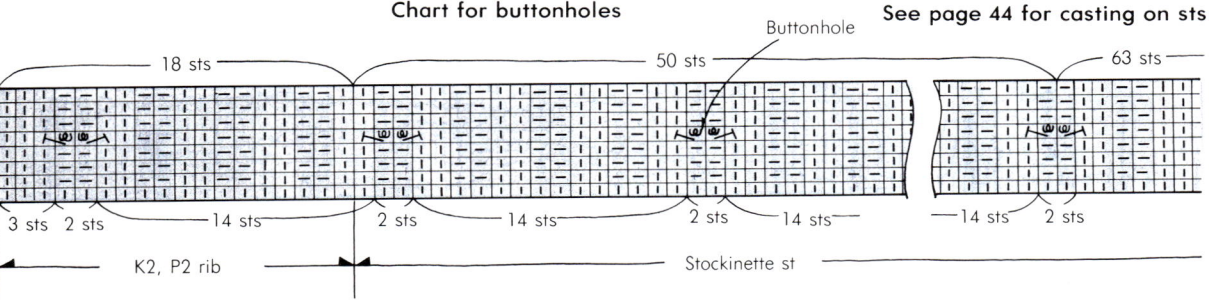

Chart for buttonholes

See page 44 for casting on sts.

How to sew on emblem

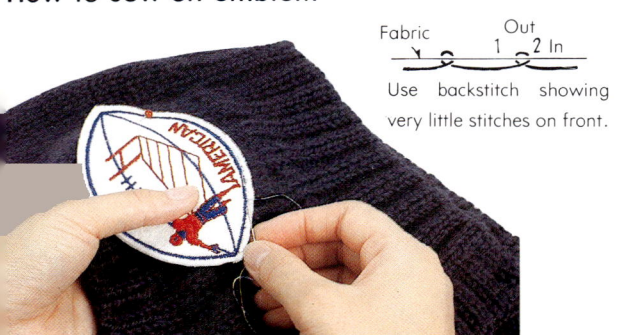

Use backstitch showing very little stitches on front.

(4) Set sleeves in.

See page 17 for setting sleeves in.

(5) Sew on buttons and emblem.

Steam-press all over knitting.
Sew on buttons and emblem.

See page 14 for steam-pressing.

Stitch Key for Knitting

The chart shows only right side of knitting. Learn stitch symbols and the right way to knit following diagrams.

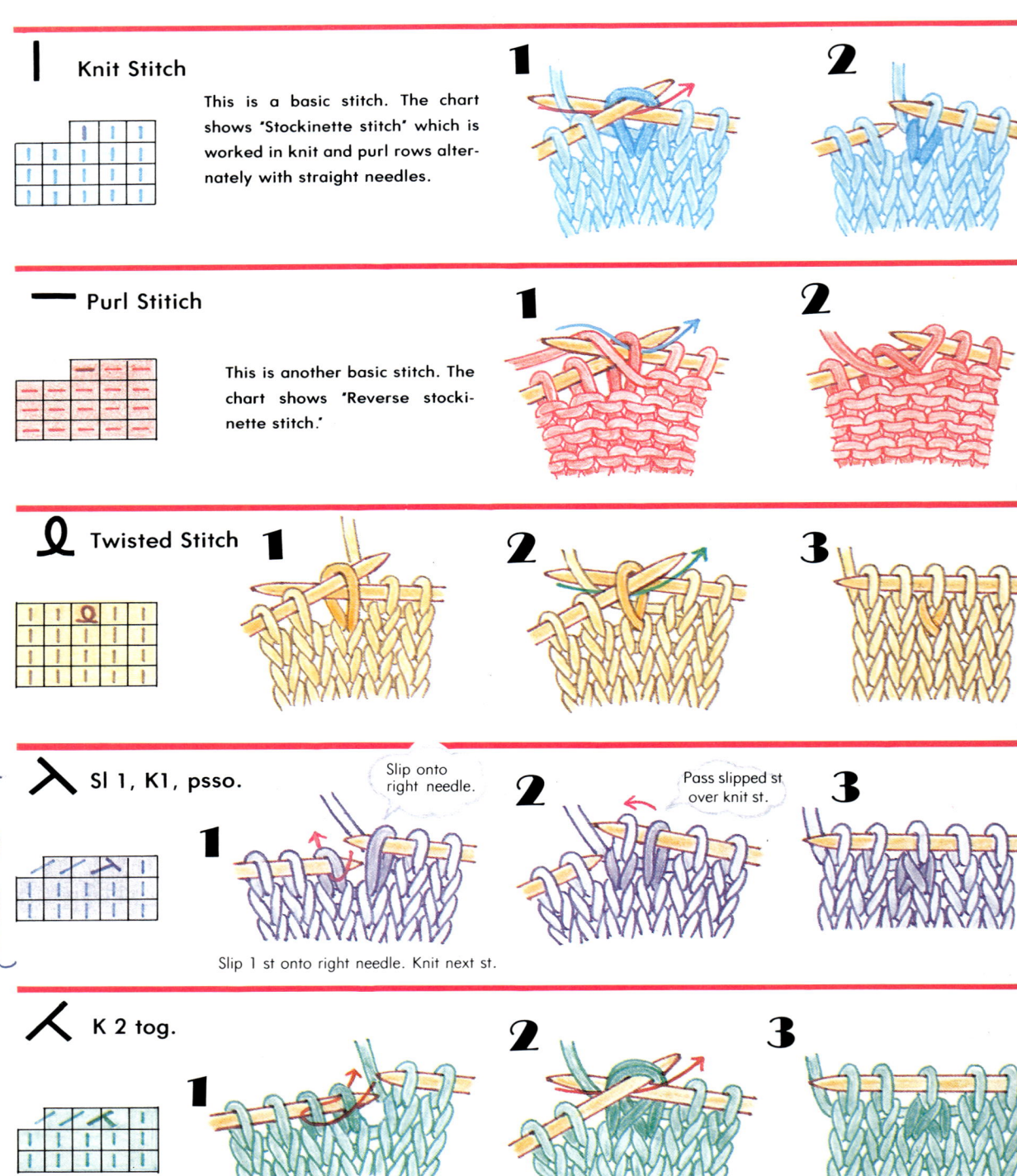

| Knit Stitch

This is a basic stitch. The chart shows 'Stockinette stitch' which is worked in knit and purl rows alternately with straight needles.

— Purl Stitch

This is another basic stitch. The chart shows 'Reverse stockinette stitch.'

Q Twisted Stitch

λ Sl 1, K1, psso.

1. Slip onto right needle. Slip 1 st onto right needle. Knit next st.
2. Pass slipped st over knit st.
3.

ʎ K 2 tog.

1. Knit 2 sts together.

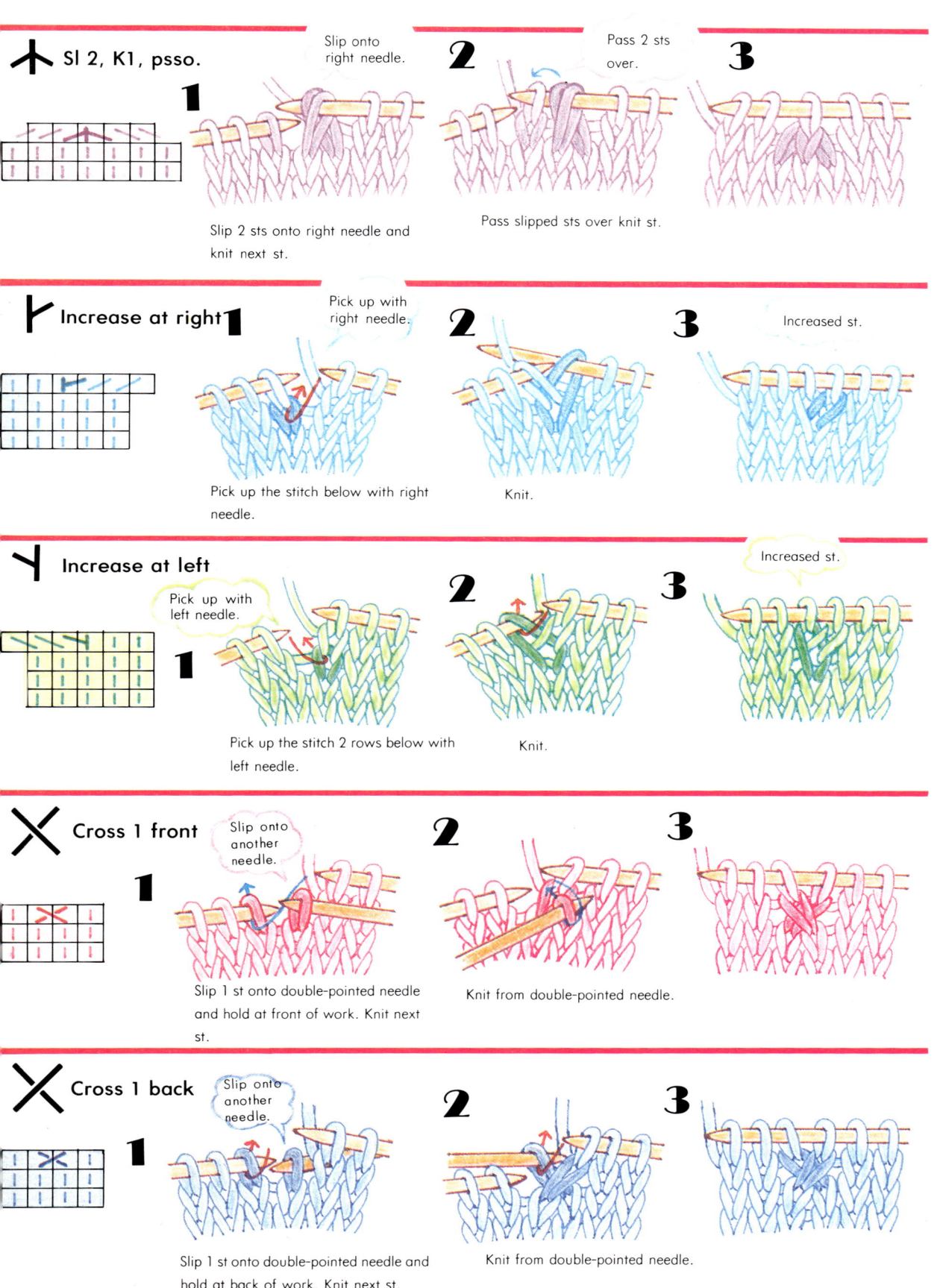

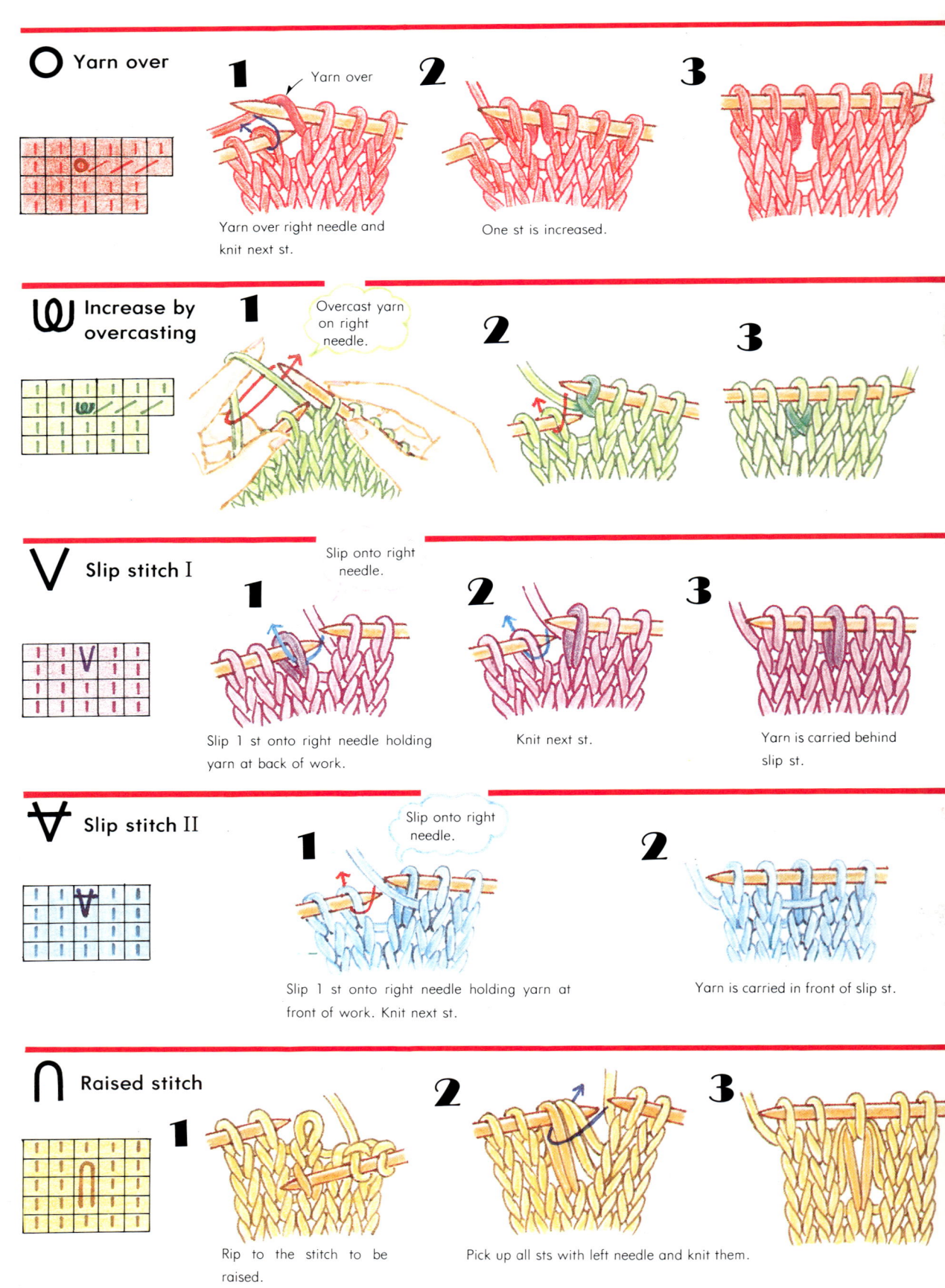